IT'S ALREADY INSIDE

PRAISES FOR *IT'S ALREADY INSIDE*

"This book is full of the wisdom needed to be an effective leader. Wisdom that reflects real life lessons, many of them very hard ones. Perhaps you are an aspiring leader? Or perhaps you have been in a leadership position for awhile, but could stand to be reminded of some of the lessons you may have forgotten? Either way, this book is a valuable read."

— **Don Wright, Ph.D.,** CEO of British Columbia Institute of Technology

"Reading this book was just as inspiring as meeting Bob in real life! He leads you with humor and wisdom to a world class level of Leadership. Not only with the brain but most importantly from the Heart."

— **Willem de Jonge,** Supply Chain Director of Heineken

"Robert Murray's book *It's Already Inside* is an engaging and humorous leadership book written by a true business veteran. Beyond vision and values, Murray delivers practical leadership advice through accounts of his own unbelievable professional experiences. His remarkable stories beg the question, "How would I have handled that?" His self-reflection questions deepen the learning and will help you apply his ideas to your own leadership practices. A must-read for all emerging leaders!"

— **Caroline de Voest,** CEO of Better Your Best Coaching

"By combing the advice and lessons of *It's Already Inside*, applying a reasonable level of competence, and having a willingness to get up, you will both kick-start and sustain a successful and rewarding career for yourself."

— **Ted Lattimore,** CEO (Retired) of Carmanah Technologies

"Robert Murray not only teaches the reader how to become a leader, but he teaches how to soar to leadership success. *It's Already Inside* is entertaining, soul-searching, and unforgettable."

— **Don Bell,** Founder and former COO of WestJet Airlines

"If you're still wondering whether you have what it takes to be a leader, well you do, and Robert Murray will make sure you know it. Robert shares stories of his amazing life here to lead you to your own Aha's—as he's done for me so many times. He shines a light on the greatness that you already have inside."

— **Nicole Donnelly,** Founder of Baby Legs, CEO of SaltyWaffle.com

"This book answers the question "What does good look like?" In fact this book is a lot of good things…a primer for developing leaders, of all ages…relevant to entrepreneurial managers, executives, and CEO's. It is full of stories for every manager that's a bit short on battle scars. And it is a good reminder for all of us with the scars! It is an easy read **and** an easy guide full of understandable references that offer humor and content and it provides 'opportunity' for a broad range of solutions both personal and professional."

— **Paul Chisholm,** CEO of IFD Corporation

"Straight forward and honest, a great book. Robert shares his thoughts on life and his personal experiences in an easy and pleasant way. The hard learning's from living and working in foreign countries but also about motivating yourself and others. It is all about you and your attitude towards life, yourself and others."

— **Bert van der Velde,** International CXO, Trainer and Coach

"Whether you're in the C-Suite of a Fortune 1000 company, or you're starting from scratch and harnessing your entrepreneurial spirit, you should read this book! Robert has captured the essence of leadership and highlighted it throughout his many personal experiences to show you that it's already inside."

— **Jeffrey Hayzlett**, Global Business Celebrity, *New York Times* Bestselling Author of *Running the Gauntlet*, Sometime Cowboy

ROBERT S. MURRAY

IT'S ALREADY INSIDE

Nurturing Your Innate Leadership for Business and Life SUCCESS

NEW YORK

It's Already Inside
Nurturing Your Innate Leadership for Business and Life Success

© 2016 Morgan James.

Published in New York, New York, by Morgan James Publishing. Morgan James and The Entrepreneurial Publisher are trademarks of Morgan James, LLC.
www.MorganJamesPublishing.com

The Morgan James Speakers Group can bring authors to your live event. For more information or to book an event visit The Morgan James Speakers Group at
www.TheMorganJamesSpeakersGroup.com.

Morgan James Publishing
The Entrepreneurial Publisher
5 Penn Plaza, 23rd Floor, New York City, New York 10001
(212) 655-5470 office • (516) 908-4496 fax
www.MorganJamesPublishing.com

9781630476250   paperback
9781630476267   eBook

Library of Congress Control Number:
2015908193

A **free** eBook edition is available
with the purchase of this print book.

CLEARLY PRINT YOUR NAME ABOVE IN UPPER CASE
Instructions to claim your free eBook edition:
1. Download the Shelfie app for Android or iOS
2. Write your name in **UPPER CASE** above
3. Use the Shelfie app to submit a photo
4. Download your eBook to any device

Cover Design by:
Rachel Lopez
www.r2cdesign.com

Interior Design by:
Brittany Bondar
www.SageDigitalDesign.com

In an effort to support local communities, raise awareness and funds, Morgan James Publishing donates a percentage of all book sales for the life of each book to Habitat for Humanity Peninsula and Greater Williamsburg.

Get involved today, visit
www.MorganJamesBuilds.com

Habitat
for Humanity®
Peninsula and
Greater Williamsburg
Building Partner

DEDICATION

This book is dedicated to:

Colleen. Proof positive that behind every successful man is a great woman. "Great" does not even begin to describe how she has always supported me with a never-ending positive outlook on our lives together. She is an amazing mother, partner, and best friend.

Denielle and Grant. Two fantastic young adults who have an amazing life in front of them because of the love and passion they have in their hearts.

Dad. The most innovative man I have ever met. He epitomizes solutions and not problems.

Countless others who help nurture my path.

To all, thank you. I am truly blessed for your love, friendship, and guidance.

I love you all.

CONTENTS

PREFACE

"A pessimist will blame the wind. An optimist expects it to change. A leader will adjust the sails."
— William Arthur Ward

Thank you for picking up this book. It represents thirty years of lessons that you can never get in a classroom. A lot of gray hair and battle scars have gone into the words in the pages in front of you. I hope it becomes your new "Pocket Leadership Mentor."

I will say this up front. I write the way I talk. After fifty some years, I am comfortable enough in my own skin to say that. I know all my English teachers and professors will be annoyed and some purists out there may be offended by my sentence structure. So be it. In business and in leadership, it really is about getting the job done. From the head and the heart. And that is where my writing comes from.

This book is laid out in short chapters that are designed to get you thinking about you, your development, and leadership. My recommendation is that you stop after each chapter and look inside to discover where your gaps are and what you need to do to nurture the leader within you so you can achieve more in your career and in life. I have provided a few discovery questions for you at the end of each chapter for this purpose. Please take time to think about them and jot down your answers in the space provided before you go on to the next chapter. My hope is this book and these questions will give you a self-discovery experience—not just a reading one.

The age-old question in business is, "Are leaders born or made?"

I get asked this question all the time. I believe that everything you need to be a great leader is already inside. It's in your DNA.

For hundreds of thousands of years, man has developed and evolved from countless challenges he has faced. During that time, our ancestors have learned and passed on to their offspring, both genetically and through teaching, the skills we all need to become leaders.

I also believe that the leadership talent, which is innate within us, needs nurturing and practice to bring out. However, remember, everything you need is already inside.

Business schools are, for the most part, teaching from a curriculum that is over a hundred years old. Professors do more telling than asking. Complicate that with young students and future leaders who have grown up in a world where they have access to instant information via computers and the Internet. No longer do children have to grow up in a world where they have to gather some cardboard boxes, pots and pans, tape, crayons, blankets, and pillows to play at make believe with their friends.

The results? Lost is the ability to think critically when new leaders arrive at the workplace. Problem finders are everywhere. Innovative problem solvers are rare. Imagination and thinking outside the box is scarce.

This book is a collection of stories about amazing leadership lessons; those lessons are imperative to all developing leaders who aspire to running their own businesses, cultivating their careers, or becoming senior executives someday. In these pages, I will share critical lessons I received from insightful mentors, world-class leaders, bosses I would follow anywhere, and bosses who were completely incompetent.

These lessons are meant to bring out the leader within you, and with focus and practice, they will imbed replicable leadership habits so they become second nature to you. With great leadership skills, you will be positioned for success in virtually any career, any situation.

I started my path being an average kid growing up in a middle class Canadian family with farming roots. We were a "blue-collar" family of seven with very little money. My upbringing pushed me toward becoming a tradesman. And that is what I did. After high school and a brief attempt at being a hockey player, I indentured as an electrician and spent all of my twenties working with my hands as an industrial electrician while my wife, Colleen, went to university and emerged as a registered nurse.

I love people who work in trades. They can solve problems without any apparent effort—a skill that I see most business people struggle with. Tradesmen also excel at working in teams versus most senior executives I have come to know who spend way too much time trying to get ahead at the expense of those around them. The problem solving I learned by being a tradesman for ten years laid the foundation for my business life as a leader.

I did not enjoy the work aspect of being an electrician. I did not find it fulfilling day in and day out—I needed more—so at thirty years old, I went to college, enrolling in night school to get my marketing degree. I loved it! I found something that challenged me in ways I had never realized. Very soon, I found opportunities to get into marketing roles—first very junior product management jobs, but soon, a very fast career growth started to accelerate. Every day was a learning experience for me in business, leadership, and life.

Promotions started happening quickly and regularly. By the time I was thirty-nine years old, I was leading a $200 million business.

All along, I was focused on being a student in leadership (I still am).

Today, I am known as a "turn-around" guy for having taken on over eighteen projects in many different countries where the businesses needed minor strategic tweaking or were in danger of complete failure.

I've had some remarkable successes along the way, but they were all successes because of the team I had working with me. The failures were because of me. That is the essence of leadership. When times are good, look out the window at your team. When times are less than good, look in the mirror because world-class leaders always take ultimate responsibility. And, great leaders encourage every leader in the organization to push boundaries, knowing full well that mistakes will be made, lessons will be learned, and employees, customers, and shareholders will prosper because of it.

I hope the chapters ahead will make you laugh, and that some will bring tears to your eyes. All have leadership lessons you cannot get in school. You can only get these lessons on the street by doing. They are my gift to you from all my battle scars received along the way in my journey of "nurturing the leader within me." My wish is for you to take these lessons, put them into practice, and become hugely successful—however you define success.

Read, learn, practice, grow, and lead. I look forward to hearing about your achievement stories as a leader.

Robert Murray
March 2015

CHAPTER 1

Is Your Character Contagious?

"There is little difference in people, but that little difference makes a big difference. The little difference is attitude. The big difference is whether it is positive or negative." — W. Clement Stone

A true leader's attitude is, as they say, unshakeable. It's contagious. When true leaders hear the word "problem," they think "solution!" When they see or feel frustration, they immediately turn their thinking around to "opportunity!"

I have often been asked, "Does anything ever get you down?" My answer very quickly is "No, nothing."

When I started eighth grade, I entered Mary Hill Junior Secondary School in Port Coquitlam—a suburb of Vancouver. There I met an amazing person—

one who has had a lasting and profound impact on my outlook on life and the curve balls that sometimes get thrown at me.

I was a hockey player. I took everything about the game seriously, particularly my preparation to be the best I could be. I had to. I am no giant by any stretch, so to survive at an elite level for my age, I had to be faster and better skilled than the goliaths I found myself around on the ice. Therefore, to keep myself in peak shape, I joined the high school cross-country running team.

Each morning, I would show up at the school for an extra run at 7:00 a.m. I would enter a dark and very quiet school and make my way to the gym to get changed for my morning run. As I walked the deserted hallways and got closer to the gym, I would start to hear the thump, thump, thump of a basketball against the floor. It would get louder and louder as I approached. I could now hear the squeak of running shoes on the hardwood, more dribbling, and a ball hitting the backboard. As I opened the door, the gym would be dark except for one end where a grade 9 student named Terry would already be shooting baskets. He would stop, look over, and with an ear-to-ear smile, yell out, "Good morning!" And go back to shooting baskets.

It was bad enough that I was there, out of a warm bed two hours early for a run in the cold, wet mornings we get on the West Coast, but Terry lived two miles from school, so he ran to school each day carrying his books and basketball. Near as I could figure, he was getting up every day at 5 a.m. or earlier. And, he was still happy!

In class, he was the guy who always received good marks, and although a bit introverted, he laughed and joked around constantly, and he would be there to help you with homework if you needed it.

After school when my cross-country teammates and I would be heading out for our afternoon workout, he would be in the gym shooting baskets. After an hour or so of our coach putting us through various forms of torture, we would be dragging our butts back to the school for a shower and home. When we came into the gym, Terry would stop to ask us how the workout went. We would grumble something incomprehensible about how Coach Tinck was killing us. Terry would smile and tell us it was good for us. At 6 p.m., he would still be there, shooting hoops after our shower; we would be heading home.

Terry would join the basketball team in late fall. The basketball coach had a policy that if you showed up for every practice, you would dress for every game. You might not play, but you got to dress. My friend was not overly tall and he was skinny—I think there was more meat on a pencil. He was not the best of players so he spent that entire first season on the bench, handing out towels and water to the guys coming off the court. That never, ever discouraged him. He always had something good to say to every player who came back to the bench.

The next year, the same routine before and after school made Terry marginally better, so the basketball coach would put him in the game if the team were ahead on the scoreboard.

The year after that, Terry made the starting line-up. He was still not tall, but the hours and hours of hard work and perseverance were starting to pay-off. As a starting guard for the team, he had the same infectious, positive attitude that was unshakeable.

In the final year of high school, Terry was recognized as the top athlete in our school along with his best friend Doug Alward—the most revered acknowledgment among a hundred or so athletes in our school. Still, he was forever grateful and would always try to deflect the attention to others. He finished academically near the top of the class. He was someone who shaped my adolescence by giving me a positive outlook—no matter what came along.

Along came college. Terry decided to go to Simon Fraser University near Vancouver. He was a "walk-on" to the university's basketball tryouts. Although he had finally put on some weight in muscle, he was not invited to the team because of his height. Surrounded by behemoths on full scholarships from across the country, Terry brought his daily work ethic and determination to every practice. At the end of the tryouts, he was designated as the Junior Varsity team's starting shooting guard. An amazing feat considering the talent that surrounded him! I was so very proud of how he once again showed everyone that through a positive mental image and a tenacious drive, anything is possible.

At the end of his first season, Terry finally went to see the doctor about a nagging knee injury that just would not heal. The doctor ran some tests, took some x-rays, and sent him to a specialist. More tests. The final diagnosis sounded like a shot heard around our little world: Bone cancer. Within days, Terry was hospitalized to have his right leg amputated above the knee.

My friend, my inspiration, if you have not already guessed, was Terry Fox—now arguably one of Canada's most famous citizens for what was to come next.

Our circle of athletic friends was crushed. This kind of event wasn't supposed to happen to someone at age eighteen—let alone someone like Terry!

Terry Fox (1980)

The evening after Terry's surgery to remove his leg, I was in his hospital room with a couple of my close friends and about twenty other friends and colleagues from school. It is a moment forever etched in my mind. The mood was somber. Teenage boys are short on words at the best of times, but this was….What could you say? "It's okay, Terry; you will be all right." What a bunch of crap, I thought. This isn't happening! This is so unfair! My head was pounding from all the screaming I was doing inside my thoughts. We all just stood there and stared at the floor, tears rolling down our cheeks.

Then, right on cue, Terry started to do what he had always done. He started talking about what was going on and how he was going to fight the cancer that temporarily sidelined him—how he had already talked to a guy at the university who played wheelchair basketball (a guy who turned out to be Rick Hansen—another very famous Canadian because of Terry's inspiration). Terry had also read an article that afternoon in the magazine *Runner's World* about a one-legged runner. Terry was doing it again. He was cheering us up, infecting us with his contagious positive attitude!

We left the hospital that evening with mixed emotions. I remember every bump in the road as we drove home. Surreal. One moment my eyes were filled with tears; the next, I was smiling in wonderment and disbelief. Here was the finest person and athlete I had ever met, struck down in his prime. "This sucks!" I thought. "It is so unfair!"

On the drive home and through the sleepless night, Terry never left my thoughts. He amazed me again and again.

Terry entered cancer treatment right away. Throughout the time he spent healing from losing his leg, including his enduring painful and debilitating chemotherapy, he remained positive and continued to inspire everyone around him. Then, in the midst of it all, he got a tutor so he could catch up on his studies and write the finals for his first year at college. Every day, the news about Terry that reached us left us stunned and amazed.

Sure he had bad days—but they were mostly brought on by people who felt sorry for him.

Soon Terry was out of the hospital, and he got fitted for a prosthetic leg. As he got stronger, he learned how to walk and very quickly he started experimenting with running. The artificial legs of the late 1970s were not meant for running so he had to develop an unusual "hop and step" style. He looked awkward, but just like Terry, he not only got the job done, but he got better and better at running.

Once again, he shocked us all by announcing one day that he was going to run across Canada and raise money for cancer research. And, once again, we thought he was crazy, but no one doubted he would do it.

After some frustrating attempts to get some corporate sponsorship, Terry and his best friend, Doug Alward, headed across the country to Newfoundland, and on a cold April 12th morning in 1980, he dipped his artificial leg into the Atlantic Ocean and started his run.

Early in Terry's run, he attracted the very rare interested supporter. It was mostly, "You won't believe this, but I just saw a one legged runner out on the highway!"

Seven days a week, Terry would average 42 kilometers (26 miles) per day (The equivalent of a full 26.2 marathon) in stages. That would be no small feat for a two legged, world-class runner, let alone a guy with one leg and a prosthetic that was not meant for running! Being a marathon runner myself, I know how tough it is. I cannot imagine doing it every single day!

Terry ran against all obstacles beyond his handicap along the way—passing cars that tried to run him off the road, lack of attention from the media, miserable weather, unbearable pain. Yet through it all, he kept going!

Once Terry crossed into the province of Ontario, people finally started to pay more attention. Terry became the viral darling of the country. The media woke up and started to cover him and his story in a big way. He started to receive a non-stop stream of invitations for appearances and meetings. Through it all, Terry kept up his average 42 kilometers a day and never refused an interview or appearance. I remember observing from afar on the West Coast how impossible his schedule seemed to be, but at the same time, thinking "That is so Terry."

Terry pushed onward. As he passed the nation's capital and then Toronto, his countrywide popularity became larger than life. He kept going. He battled through pain, blisters on his stump and on his good foot. He kept going.

Just as he was past the halfway point of his Marathon of Hope (as it became known), Terry ended a run early one morning, crawled into his bed in the back of his support van, and told Doug he needed to see a doctor. He had been battling severe pain, congestion, and coughing in his chest for close to a month, and on this day, he had no energy left in his tank. The prognosis from the doctor and the hospital was that the cancer had come back and spread to his lungs.

Terry's run was over. He had run 3,339 miles in 143 days.

In true Terry Fox fashion, he made a tearful apology to everyone who had supported him and to the nation. He vowed that he would not give up the fight so he could return one day and finish the journey. It was a speech that ripped my heart out and the hearts of everyone watching.

Terry came home and began treatment again. It soon became evident that the treatment was not working. Terry became weaker and sicker.

The last time I saw Terry was two months before his death in April, 1981. A group of friends and I were together one night at a local watering hole enjoying a Friday night beer. Terry walked into the bar, and as if by some divine presence, the entire place went silent. Terry came over to our table, sat down, and ordered a beer. We were stunned. He had shriveled away to half of his former size. The cancer ravaging his body was clearly winning.

In true Terry Fox fashion, he started talking about life and what it meant to have lived the life he had. Soon we were all telling jokes and laughing. Right to the end, Terry's attitude was unshakeable. It was truly worth catching!

Terry's original vision for his Marathon of Hope was to raise the equivalent of one dollar from every Canadian to enable cancer research for a cure (about

$23 million). Today, there are Terry Fox runs annually in 60 countries around the world. To date, the legacy of Terry Fox has raised over $550 million. Cancer research and cures have moved leaps and bounds ahead of where they were in 1980. The lung cancer that took Terry is treatable today because of the research his foundation has funded.

For me, I like to think of my attitude as unshakable. The lessons I acquired from Terry in the eight short years I knew him have served me beyond anything else I have ever learned. My positive, can-do attitude that I have fashioned after Terry's has enabled me to take on some of the toughest leadership challenges. I have learned to lead with vision, purpose, and optimism—to enable those around me to see solutions and opportunity instead of problems and hopelessness.

On really tough days, when it is dark and cold outside, and I am tired and just want to hit the "snooze alarm" five times, I think of Terry and I start to move. My feet hit the floor, and one step after another, I get back in the game. I hold my head up high and remember that I am a leader and people around me depend on me to do the right thing and be there for them.

Discover what gets you out of bed in the morning and get out there and be the world's best at what you do. If you need motivation, just Google "Terry Fox" and see for yourself what I was incredibly blessed to experience!

The cool part is that you can choose your attitude. You can choose to make your attitude unshakeable and contagious!

What gets you out of bed in the morning?

What gets you excited about what you do and keeps you doing it?

How are you going to ensure that you live a life by your design?

What makes you optimistic about the future?

CHAPTER 2

The "Roof of Africa"—Vision and Leadership Lessons from the Most Unlikely Sources

"Don't be afraid of the space between your dreams and reality. If you can dream it, you can make it so." — Belva Davis

I am standing on a ridge at an altitude of 4,500 meters and looking across the high desert plain at Mount Kilimanjaro. After four long days of climbing, "Kili" is only 10 kilometers (6 miles) away, but from here, it feels like it will take a lifetime to reach.

My head and chest are in intense pain—worse than anything I have ever felt. I have no energy. I don't feel like doing anything!

"What am I doing here?" I silently ask myself.

Then I hear it. "Ten Up and Ten Down!" yells one of my team members. One by one, our spirits lift and we refocus on the goal; surprisingly, I put one foot in front of the other and start moving.

The View from 10 Kilometers Away

What does this scene have to do with Vision, Mission, Values, Strategy, Execution, and Leadership?

For you to understand, I have to take you back six days to the beginning....

I had been working in Romania as an executive with Vodafone, and my wife and children were there with me, but they had decided to return home to Vancouver for the summer. I decided to take advantage of their absence by having an adventure. On July 1st, 2006, I flew from Romania to Kilimanjaro to fulfill a dream to climb one of the highest peaks in the world. I picked "Kili" because I figured it was the only peak of that altitude (5,895 meters or 19,160 feet) that is not a technical climb. Kilimanjaro is located in Tanzania just 3 degrees south of the equator. It rises majestically out of the jungle.

Below it, Africa's wildest animals roam and the locals eke out an existence growing bananas and coffee.

July 1st came way too fast. For months I had been lazily training for my climb—thinking it was "just a trek" and would not be technical. "How hard can it be?" I thought. I never could have been more wrong!

Four months earlier, I had been part of an eight-man group of ex-pat executives from Bucharest who were going to make the climb. The "Dream" had started a year earlier with a bunch of guys I was running with on Sundays. Anyway, as life would have it, the guys started dropping out for various reasons (hang nail, family reunion, had to wash his hair, etc.)

I decided to carry on and go it alone.

The flight to the postage stamp of an airstrip at Kilimanjaro International Airport with KLM took ten hours. The beauty was that Kili is in the same time zone as Romania so there was no jet lag. The airport consisted of this tiny little paved strip of a runway (it must have been an aviator's nightmare to set down there the massive Boeing 777 we were in) and a small tin-roofed shack that was the terminal building. The doors of the plane opened and 350 people filed out onto the tarmac and into the Customs area, which was hot, humid, and mosquito infested. To top it off, only one Customs Agent was on duty to sell entry visas and process everyone's paperwork. I was in the middle of the pack, and it took me two hours to get through it all. The good news, of course, was that I did not have to wait for my baggage once I cleared Customs.

Finally, out of the airport and on the ground in Tanzania, I was met by the tour company representative and was loaded into a Land Rover for the three hour drive over what was supposed to be a road to the base of Mount Kilimanjaro.

Stepping Outside the Kilimanjaro Airport to See "Kili" in the Distance

When I checked into the Kibo Hotel at 11 p.m., I was looking forward to a good night's sleep after a very long day of travelling. After the clerk at the desk gave me this massive skeleton key, I made my way through a thick garden to my room, which from the outside, looked like a very small tool shed.

Remember this part for the end of this story! I inserted the key into the lock, turned it, and the lock made this very authoritarian "Clunk" as it freed the door from the latch. The door creaked open and I reached inside for the light switch. Nothing. I opened my duffle bag and felt around for my flashlight. Flicking on the flashlight revealed a small room that very much looked like it was outfitted from the local prison surplus shop. Small bed, paper thin mattress draped with a mosquito net, and a prison issue toilet (Read: a hole in the ground) that doubled as a drain for the handheld shower sprayer thingy hanging from the wall. A bedside lamp had no shade—just a naked bulb. There were two windows in the room, but neither one of them had glass—just metal mesh mortared into the cement walls. I rolled my sleeping bag out onto the bed and crawled inside the netting while thinking I was about to sleep like a baby. Wrong!

Soon after I switched the light out, it started. Something in the room with multiple legs and built like a Chicago Bears linebacker started marching around inside the room. Mosquitoes buzzed in formation like Stuka dive-bombers, each taking turns peeling off and making a strafing run at my mosquito netting. Just as I was dozing off from pure exhaustion, the rooster in the henhouse next to my room decided to wake all of Africa at 4:00 a.m. This sound set off a chain reaction of neighboring testosterone burdened roosters competing for the title of the most annoying poultry of the day. Not to be outdone, all the local dogs decided to join in on the party. Ungowa! I was thinking, where is one of those groups of African Safari hunters when you need it?

Seven a.m. finally came! After breakfast, I went to the trip briefing and was introduced for the first time to the team with whom I would climb. I was grouped in with nine other climbers. A young couple from Denmark, three Irish girls who, at the young age of twenty-nine, had been all over the world on multiple adventures, three Irish lads who were raising money for children's cancer research, and my tent and climbing partner, a Lebanese-Canadian guy who worked for Phillip Morris in Lithuania.

It was a great balance between the soft-spoken, easy-going nature of the Danes, the lively zest for life of the six Irish who constantly told jokes and taught us new words, the Lebanese guy with the Canadian passport, and myself. There was instant chemistry and never a dull moment!

The guide giving us the briefing was very, very thorough—right down to the pain we would be in as we gained more altitude toward the peak—and the severe temperatures, the wind, the exhaustion, and how the guide team would evacuate us from the mountain in an emergency. I was sitting there thinking, "Great, I paid how much for this again? I am supposed to be on vacation here!" The Irish guys were saying, "Great, a whole week without beer. This sucks!"

We were told that only 50 percent of those who attempt the peak make it (on the tour company's Web site, it says 87 percent who attempt the climb make it—I guess the 37 percent is the difference between Operations and Marketing!). Women and asthmatics stand a better chance of making it than do most very fit men—women because they can produce red blood cells faster than men (critical for dealing with oxygen deprivation), and asthma sufferers because they are better at dealing with lack of oxygen.

After the briefing, we all had to submit our equipment to an inspection to ensure we had warm enough clothing and sleeping bags and adequate personal emergency supplies. Once all were approved, we were off to waiting Land Rovers for the two-hour drive around the base of the mountain to our starting point.

The ride was over very rough, red volcanic dirt roads through the jungle and many villages. Each village we came across, the road would be lined with hundreds of children smiling and waving at us as we drove by. It was amazing—they had nothing, but they were always happy looking and clean. A cultural and regional note: Tanzanians have large families—often five kids or more. Fifty percent of Tanzanian adults have HIV or full-blown AIDS. Not until 2005 did the Tanzanian Government finally admit to the general population that unprotected sex caused the spread of HIV and AIDS. Until then, the Minister of Health was telling people that HIV was not a sexually transmitted disease. As we drove through these villages, I couldn't help but think of the millions of orphans there will be in the coming years.

Two Tanzanian children stand by the road as our procession drives by.

So much for clean clothes! When we arrived at the launching point for the climb, we were all covered from top to toe with a thick layer of red dust from the roads. Our hair was red, our eyelashes were red, and one Irish lad's teeth were even red because he had spent the whole trip smiling! We were at 1,900 meters in elevation; the hot humid air from the airport the night before was now replaced with cool, dryer air, and NO BUGS! We were still in jungle-type vegetation with thick foliage and the occasional monkey peering out to look at the new batch of "Whities."

It was here that we met the entire support team. Our climbing team would be supported by the head guide (whom we had already met), three assistant guides, a summit porter (whose job was to be last in the procession and collect any dead bodies), a head cook (This man turned out to be a genius! The meals he prepared were amazing!), four helping porters (They helped the cook in camp and carried very heavy things) and twenty porters (They carried very, very heavy things!). Our support team members were all very tall, very sinewy, with skin blacker than coal, and when they smiled, which was all the time, their teeth were whiter than snow! Their personal belongings for the week fit into a very small backpack (Strange, I thought, because of the freezing temperatures we had been warned about). Each porter carried a supply load of 40 kilos (90 pounds) of other equipment from tents, cooking equipment, and food to our personal equipment—and they carried it gracefully in large packages upon their heads! We "tourists," carried a backpack consisting of our clothes for the day, 6 liters of water (drinking massive amounts of water is the number one defense against altitude sickness—I ended up drinking about 10 liters of water each day and going into the bush every twenty minutes to relieve myself) and our emergency supplies. The sum total of the weight that my sorry ass would haul each day was 20 pounds!

The porters set off up the trail through the jungle with us following closely behind. After five minutes, they were gone. All twenty-four of the porters with their 100 pounds of extra stuff vanished in the distance. Meanwhile, we plodded along under the watchful eyes of our guides, stopping occasionally to take pictures of the wildlife (giraffes, monkeys, elephants way in the distance, flamingos, baboons) and very often to pee! This part of Tanzania has no predatory animals so we never had to worry about anything with big teeth and bad breath stopping by to see how tasty we might be—although, I did remind myself of that old jungle law: "You need only be faster than the slowest member in the group!"

More "locals" check us out as we trek along.

After a relatively easy four hours of walking, we emerged from the jungle at 2,500 meters in elevation and into vegetation called "Moraine." It wasn't scrub brush and it wasn't trees either. It consisted of heather-like bushes that stood five feet tall and poinsettia (the same as the Christmas plants) bushes that stood about ten feet tall. Weird! This spot was also the site of our first camp.

The porters, who had left us in the dust four hours earlier, had completely set up camp. Our tents were set up. Two cook tents and a mess tent were complete. Water had been fetched, boiled, and was now sitting in cooling pots awaiting our empty camel packs for re-fills. The smell of dinner was wafting in the air and tea and cookies were ready—as if I didn't feel inadequate enough earlier, I couldn't believe what they had accomplished ahead of us!

Dinner that night was chicken vegetable soup, fresh fish, grilled vegetables and potatoes, fresh bread, fresh mango, and pound cake. It was amazing! We ate like we had been adrift on a raft for weeks. The cool, thin mountain air made for big appetites.

Sitting around with the team in the mess tent after dinner, our group got a chance to talk together for the first time since we had met twelve hours earlier. We were from four different cultures. Among us were a marketing executive, a student, a journalist, two civil engineers, a middle manager, a medical lab technician, a teacher, a librarian, and myself—a sales executive doing a turn-around in Romania for Vodafone.

What was absolutely amazing about our group were the richness of the questions and the profoundness of the answers. For a time, I sat quietly and listened intently—blown away by what was unfolding in front of me. The conversations started to map out what we, as business leaders, would pay thousands of dollars to a consulting firm to facilitate!

My new teammates were asking things like:

- What do you think it will feel like to stand on the top of Kilimanjaro?
- Will we all make it?
- How will you feel if you do not make it?

The answers I heard (from people with different lives, different circumstances, different cultures) were passionate, full of energy, and vibrant in detail. Obviously, we each had been thinking about this trip for a very long time. After only a few minutes, it dawned on me that my new teammates were describing their own personal visions. The '"what" for where they were currently going with their lives.

Equally amazing was that no one got hung up on "not making it" to the top of the mountain. For them, optimism seemed to abound—something I find frequently in people who have prepared for and lived for something in their minds for a long time.

The conversations then blended into a simple sentence that summarized how connected we had become with each other in half a day, and what we wanted to achieve by the end of the week. We were ten in number, so "Ten Up and Ten Down" became our mantra.

"Wow!" I thought. "Ten Up and Ten Down." This was our vision as a group. Like all great vision statements, it was simple, straightforward, clear, and compelling! It instantly gave us all a common focus.

Every successful leader and his or her respective successful business needs to have a clear and compelling vision of "What Good Looks Like" in order to motivate and inspire a team to move toward a goal that, in the beginning, seems challenging and maybe even unattainable. My disparate teammates and I had, in a few short minutes, without the help of consultants, mapped out a vision worthy of framing on the boardroom wall!

It didn't stop there. Right on cue, I next heard questions like:

- What is important to you?
- If you could take one thing to the top of the mountain, what would it be?

Incredible! Personal values were coming out. And as in all great teams and businesses that I have been a leader of, it was easy to see common personal values and how they linked to the vision—values like integrity, loyalty, determination, love for family and friends, passion, fun, and living life to the max!

The banter was that easy, but still startling to me as a business leader who knows how important it is to have a vision aligned with values; otherwise, achievement is futile.

The exchange then shifted to questions about:

- Why do you want to do this?
- Why Kilimanjaro?

You just can't script stuff like this! Purpose. Mission. The "Why" in our "What's." What drives people to do what they do? In business, a vision is just words on the wall unless the organization knows exactly what it wants to be known for among its team members and in the communities it serves.

Our team had purpose and it aligned seamlessly with our vision (Ten Up and Ten Down) and our values. We never said, "Okay, let's wordsmith these thoughts into a Mission Statement." But nonetheless, our mission was as clear as the millions of stars that now dotted the sky.

On our trek, we committed to helping each other with whatever support we needed—morally or physically. Now, adventure climbing is also fraught with life's realities, and sometimes, in order for a team to be the most successful it can be, people have to be left behind. So we came to an agreement, that, if any one of us was not capable of carrying on, the team would not make the decision to leave that person behind—the person incapable or too sick to climb would do so.

Dumbfounded by the structure and organization that, so unconsciously, had just come to life, I chuckled to myself, "All that's missing now is a set of strategies for how all this is going to happen?" The "how" for delivering our "what": The Vision.

No sooner had that thought crossed my mind than someone said, "How are we going to do this?" Then I got a serious case of "trout mouth" (a look similar to a fish with its mouth wide open)!

Thoughts started to flow, and before I knew it, we had four key strategies for how we were going to achieve our vision:

1. **Climb High and Sleep Low:** To combat altitude sickness, climbers will often climb up higher each day than they need to, and then climb back down to a lower altitude to make camp for the night.
2. **Eat While You Can:** To be successful when your body is tested to the maximum, you need to have plenty of energy reserves. Altitude sickness destroys your appetite and in some cases makes you unable to keep food down—so eat while you can and as often as you can.
3. **Clear and Copious:** The number one defense against altitude sickness is being fully hydrated. High altitudes (like the ones we were venturing into), require you to take in 8 to 10 liters of water per day. "Clear and Copious" simply meant that if you were drinking enough water, you would have to stop every twenty minutes to, well, you know, pee. And your pee should be clear colored and plentiful (copious).
4. **Slowly, Slowly:** We would only move as fast as the slowest member of the group. We agreed that in order to achieve "Ten Up and Ten Down," everyone needed to have the strength to do it, and no one should be taxed of energy by trying to keep up with the faster members of the group.

There it was. The model that successful businesses all over the world use was now complete. I was stunned! It dawned on me that business and leadership is really simple stuff complicated by idiots. Ten people from different backgrounds had just completed in one hour of conversation what some businesses struggle with even after going away for a "Management Team Building" meeting for three days with facilitators to craft the strategic plan!

No one assumed the leadership position. We had no power struggles—no politics and no ulterior motives. Just ten people from different walks of life with a common purpose, aligned with their values and a clear vision.

The altitude also made for an early bedtime. Because Tanzania is almost on the equator, the sun sets every day of the year at precisely 7:00 p.m. and rises at 7:00 a.m. I crawled into my sleeping bag at 8:00 that night and was out cold until our guides woke us the next morning at 6:30 by serving us tea in bed. I later mentioned to my wife, Colleen, that it would be nice to have tea in bed every morning at home. She said, "Sure, if you sleep out in the yard every night in a tent, I'll bring you tea the next morning."

Then it was out of the tent to a waiting pan of hot water to, as our guides would say, "Washy, washy!"

As we all, one-by-one, rolled out of our tents, we would stand and see Kilimanjaro in the distance, highlighted by the rising sun. Incredible! One-by-one, we would each take turns repeating our mantra, "Ten Up and Ten Down," just as successful business leaders everywhere do to motivate their teams by repeatedly focusing them on the vision and where they are going. Vision is like brushing your teeth—it has to be done daily!

Breakfast would be waiting too. Every morning we would walk into the mess tent to find hot oatmeal, ham and eggs, toast, and fresh mango and melon. After breakfast, we packed up our personal belongings, loaded up with another 6 liters of water, a bag of cookies, chocolate bars and bananas, and headed off with Kilimanjaro calling in the distance. We would remind each other about our strategies, look up at Kili, and say, "She's waiting." We would trek off, leaving the porters behind with dirty dishes and the entire camp to take down and pack up. Life is hard in the African outback!

Five minutes into the second day, our lead guide suddenly screamed "Buffalo!" and dove 90 degrees into the bush. The ten of us stood there like deer caught in the headlights until we heard what sounded like approaching thunder bearing down the trail. When the ground started to shake, our tight pack of ten fearless adventurers started running backwards—that is, of course, until the guy at the back tripped and fell, causing a domino chain reaction! Whatever was headed our way, it was big, and luckily, it veered off into the bush before it could play ten pin bowling with the dumbfounded tourists! As the thunder rolled off into the distance, our guide rolled out of the bush, brushed himself off, and nonchalantly said, "Okay. Let's go." One of the Irish lads replied, "Not until I go change my shorts!"

About forty minutes later, the porters we had left behind with all the camp to clean up and break down, passed us like we were standing still. More battering to our egos!

Porters passing us (again)! Mount Kilimanjaro looming in the foreground.

We hiked for four hours and arrived at a lava field, where multiple large caves had been formed a million years ago from previous volcanic explosions. There we found the porters with tables set up (complete with tablecloths and napkins), water fetched and boiled, and lunch ready for us. Another three course hot meal and we were off for four more hours of hiking. And yes, forty-five minutes after leaving the lunch stop, the porters passed us again!

This became our daily routine. We steadily gained altitude. We would hike 8-11 hours and cover a total distance of 70 kilometers in six days.

Camp Two was at 3,600 meters where the vegetation changed to alpine desert.

Camp Three was at 4,200 meters in the crater of an extinct volcano where there was no vegetation—just an eerie moonscape.

Camp Four was at 4,700 meters at the foot of Kilimanjaro's final steep ascent. As we climbed, the temperature dropped and the wind picked up. Mornings would be -5 to -20 Celsius (23 to -4 Fahrenheit), and the wind was always blowing, making it feel colder (which made middle of the night pee breaks very painful), especially since my sleeping bag was so hot that I was always sleeping in my boxers).

Every morning our unconscious leadership ritual would start. At waking and crawling out of the tent, we would each look up at the mountain and visualize what it would be like to stand on the top. At breakfast, someone would always say, "Ten Up and Ten Down."

As we loaded our packs for the day, we would always review our four strategies. Not in a military, checklist kind of way, but by asking each other how we felt:

- Do you think you drank enough yesterday?
- Did you eat enough?
- How much higher do you want to climb today before coming back down?

- Was the pace okay yesterday?

Regular strategic plan review is how the top companies in the world execute flawlessly.

We would, again unconsciously, break down the vision into small, bite-sized pieces—baby steps so to speak, so we would not get overwhelmed by the sheer size of the task—just like world-class leaders do to inspire their teams to execute step-by-step.

Throughout the day's climb, we would constantly check in with each other about pace, water, food, and how each of us was feeling. In business, we call this measuring and inspecting. Critical to execution!

At the end of each day, we would celebrate at dinner by recognizing each other for continuing to push on, even though some team members were starting to get very sick. It was eerily similar to how top business leaders recognize their teams for achievements and motivate them to take it to the next level.

Vision and Strategy really is a daily event!

Altitude sickness crept in very slowly. On day three when we broke through 4,000 meters, it started with a feeling like being hung-over: first, a dull headache, followed by a lack of energy. From there, the headache got more and more intense until at Camp Four, I thought my eyes were going to pop out. My ears ached. My nose bled. My pulse rate, which normally at rest is 48-50, crept up to 70-80. When I would do something strenuous, like bend over to tie up my boots, my pulse would be 120. Something really strenuous like walking and my pulse would be 160-180. Each and every beat of my heart made my head hurt even more. Others in our group became so nauseated that they started to throw up every time they ate.

On day four, where this story began, we spent eight hours hiking 10 kilometers across a flat, desolate landscape before we arrived at our last ascending camp. The wind was cold and dry—whipping lava dust at us that choked our already labored breathing and stung against any exposed skin. We sheltered each other by walking in a tight group. We talked the entire time to keep each other from thinking about the pain; we talked about what it was going to be like standing on the top, about our favorite movies, songs, and books, about the pro's and con's of the current U.S. president. Anything except talking about quitting.

We finally arrived at Camp Four, elevation 4,700 meters, at 4 in the afternoon. We were exhausted, cold, in pain, and sick.

Our briefing for our final assault that night on the peak was simple. Try and sleep before dinner. Get up for dinner (if you can eat) at 7:00 o'clock. Go back to bed and try to sleep. Our guides would wake us up at 11:30 p.m. with tea. We were to dress for the forecasted -20 temperature and 60 kilometer winds. At 11:50, load our packs with 6 liters of hot water (hot to keep us warm and to prevent the water from freezing), put on ski goggles, turn our head torches on, and start the final ascent at midnight. If we had waited until daylight, we would not have reached the peak until after dark the next evening; plus, we did not want to descend in the dark, since the descent would be more dangerous than the ascent.

We climbed through the night—slowly, painfully! Oh, how my head hurt! I started to lose the feeling in both of my hands and forearms ("Oh, great," I thought! "Now if I could get the two pairs of gloves off that I was wearing, how would I know whether I was successfully picking my nose or not!"). Each breath I took was long and deep. I was working so hard to breathe that every muscle in my chest started to scream. Halfway through the night, my legs started to shake—not from cold but exhaustion.

At 5:00 a.m., we lost all four of the girls in our group. They were so severely sick that they started to collapse each time they took a step. The rest of the team tried in vain to lift their spirits and encourage them to take another step, but to no avail. They were completely spent and at risk of serious injury—so they pulled the trigger on their climb as we had all agreed on the first night. Two of the assistant guides in the group spent the next four hours getting them back down to Camp Four where they could recover in the now relatively breathable 4,700 meter air.

At 7:00 a.m., the sun started to rise. What an incredible sight! I don't think I can remember a more beautiful sunrise! The clear, clean air. The clouds thousands of feet below us. And now, the clearly visible curvature of the earth made it spectacular! In the new morning daylight, we also saw for the first time what we had been climbing all night. I remember thinking that I now knew why we had climbed at night. My second thought was, "How are we going to get down?"

At 8:00 a.m., what was left of our team crested over the crater of the world's largest volcano to "Gilman's Point" at 5,600 meters. We were all exhausted beyond anything we had ever experienced—and we had all done multiple marathons between us. We snapped some pictures, and without much fanfare, we continued on toward the peak.

At 10 a.m., we arrived at 5,895 meters or 19,160 feet—the highest point in Africa. What a feeling. We were the only ones on the peak. For a few moments, the pain went away. I remember thinking how amazing the human body is when you tell yourself what you are capable of accomplishing. How powerful a vision is when it gets you to do things that scare you—that you think impossible!

The six out of ten of us who made it to the top took turns taking each other's picture. The Irish lads got onto a cell phone (yes, there was a signal up there) and did an interview with a radio station back in Dublin. I collected some rocks to take home. Our guide Samuel sat down, took off his gloves, removed the scarf that covered his face, and lit a cigarette—all in a day's work for him.

On the "Roof of Africa" flying the Canadian Flag.

We were on the peak for about twenty minutes before Samuel urged us to start down to return to breathable air. All of us were out of water and drained of energy. It had taken ten hours of non-stop climbing to get to the peak. It took three hours to get back to Camp Four. At 1:00 p.m., I collapsed into my tent with my boots and all my cold weather gear still on. In the blink of an eye, it was 2:00 p.m. and Samuel was waking us up, telling us we had to leave right away for the four hour trek down to Camp Five or we would run out of daylight. I thought he was kidding! At 6:00 p.m., we stumbled into Camp Five at 3,700 meters, having been on our feet for seventeen of the last eighteen hours. Ah, breathable air! It felt like I was breathing pure oxygen! My headache was completely gone!

Washy, washy, dinner and in bed by 7:30 that night! I never heard a single thing or remember a single thought until 7:30 the next morning when Samuel was waking us up for the last day of our trek. Day Six was a short 21 kilometers of gentle downhill, which would take us eight hours and had the enticing promise of hot showers for the first time in six days and cold beer waiting for us!

Now we were back where we began. We got to the park gate and loaded up into Land Rovers once again for the ride back to the Kibo Hotel. When I walked into the very hotel room I had one long week ago, it was paradise! I shaved (twice) and stood in the best shower I could remember having for a very long time. Then, I went to the hotel bar, and with the Irish lads, I drank some of the coldest, best tasting beer ever until the wee hours of the morning (learning even more new words from the lads as we drank). Back in my room, the bed felt like a cloud, and apparently, the roosters never crowed the next morning.

How one week can change one's perspective significantly! I had learned a lifetime of leadership lessons on the way to the "Roof of Africa," and they were leadership lessons from the most unlikely sources. What I discovered mostly though is that vision, values, and purpose are in all of us—they are a part of our lives and what make life worth chasing and living to the max!

As a leader, I recommend you discover the power of a vision. Discover how a vision for the business and even for small projects can help people wrap their heads around what success looks like. And, as a leader, you need to practice visualizing that vision every day—it really is like brushing your teeth.

Do you lead everything you do with a vision of where you are going? When you are about to lead a group, or even yourself, do you, as Stephen Covey says, "Begin with the end in mind?"

What is your personal vision? Take a few moments and write out what you want to achieve in the next five years.

Now take those thoughts and craft it into a simple statement that you are able to repeat to yourself every morning.

CHAPTER 3

"Why?" Unlock This Code and Watch What Happens!

"The greatest mistake a man can make is to be afraid of making one." — Elbert Hubbard

People will follow you virtually anywhere if they understand why. Christopher Columbus did not have hostages on his journey into unknown seas to discover the New World. He had volunteers.

As leaders, we often have access to information others have not yet had time to digest. We may have even been involved in the debate at a senior or board level over the potential solutions to a problem the business is facing. We have had the time to figure out what the situation means and why a strategy or change process needs to be implemented.

Often, our frontline teams get little or none of this information. They just get some leader standing in front of them waving his or her arms around and professing what way we are going! In a military organization, that may work since soldiers are groomed to follow orders (even if they don't make sense). In business, however, frontline people need to and want to know WHY? They want to know not only what we are going to do, and how we are going to do it, but also, why we need to do it. They want to know what it means to them personally.

John F. Kennedy gave an amazing speech to Congress in May of 1961. He captivated the imaginations of the entire nation by detailing the vision of sending a man to the moon by the end of that decade and returning him safely to earth again. At that time, the U.S. was losing the Space Race to the Russians. Americans had absolutely no idea how they were going to send a man to the moon, but President Kennedy was telling the world they were going to accomplish the feat in less than nine years.

The vision of going to the moon, however, wasn't the important thing. The Soviet Union had the same vision. What motivated and inspired the nation was the why.

The why for President Kennedy was that he feared losing the Cold War to the Soviets. He needed the nation to get back its competitive advantage, which had made the U.S. the reigning superpower. That meant the U.S. needed to return to being the top country in the world in terms of intellectual capital. In the years just prior to Kennedy's speech, a decline in enrollments in higher education—particularly, higher technical and engineering education—had happened in the United States. Kennedy believed that racing the Soviets to the moon would encourage Americans to go back into higher education and preserve the U.S.'s position as a leader and an economic superpower.

For the American people, Kennedy positioned the "why" by placing it within the competitive race over a rival superpower that threatened Americans' way of life through the Cold War threat of nuclear destruction. Winning the race to the moon was about not sitting around in fear wondering what would happen if some leader lost his mind and pushed "the button." It was about proving to the world that Americans were not going to be beaten. It worked. The whole nation rallied behind the vision. Everyone wanted to be part of it. Kennedy knew the American people had a will to win, and he used that will to get the intellectual capital of the nation going. Enrollment in higher level technical education skyrocketed.

In answering why, remember that different stakeholder groups (leaders and employees for example) can have different and very personal why's for doing something. As a leader, it is critical to figure that out and use it as the motivator in clear and compelling communications. Typically, all employees want to be part of something that matters. They want to know that their efforts and intellectual contributions are worthy and recognized. They want work that is purposeful. When you are able to achieve that, you will have reached the pinnacle of success with a team by engaging its members' hearts and minds.

I succeed in winning over teams in business by involving everyone in the early stages of strategy development and asking their opinions on how we are going to achieve the desired outcomes of the business as set for us by shareholders. I also get team members to complete this simple phrase: "I believe...."

By using this process, Apple came up with its purpose which continues today: "Think differently." That simple two-word statement drives everything done at Apple from product development to marketing. It is a key reason why Apple currently holds the dominant position in the world as an innovator. Every Apple employee thrives on being part of a company that thinks differently, and now millions of customers around the world want to be part of it too. So simple. At the end of the day, Apple is just a computer company like any other, but the difference is in its purpose and its focus on that purpose.

Similarly, Disney imbeds its purpose of "Bring Joy" in all team members, starting right at the recruiting, assessment, hiring, on-boarding, and development of every employee. This simple "why" is rooted in every "cast member" at Disney and is best exemplified by the fact that a piece of trash is never on the ground at a Disney theme park for longer than seven seconds. Cast members do not care whose job it is. If they see trash, they pick it up. It is all part of "Bringing Joy."

When your team members understand "why" you are leading them in a direction toward a yet to be seen destination, they will follow you with all their hearts.

"Why" is just as important a piece for creating happy employees as vision and strategy. It brings purpose. And purpose drives customer satisfaction, and ultimately, a profitable enterprise.

Here's a great exercise for all leaders. On a personal level, take a few moments and write out what is your WHY.

Why do you have the career aspirations you have?

Why do you live where you do?

Why do you drive the car you do?

Why do you have the personal relationships you have?

Finish off by writing your own purpose statement. Here's mine:

"To approach everyday with the highest level of consciousness, a contagious positive attitude, and exude maximum energy, enthusiasm, and passion for life and living.

To love unconditionally, and to nurture and care for my family and friends the best that I can.

To strive for optimal personal mental, physical, and spiritual health through learning, experiencing, exploring, and growing as much as I can and caring for and fueling my body the best I can.

Professionally, to deliver value and results everyday through innovation, guts, and determination. As a leader, to teach, coach, and mentor my teammates with vision, focus, integrity, honesty, and trust."

What's yours? When you can connect to your own personal WHY, it makes it easier as a leader to connect with other people's WHY and how to connect it all together in a cohesive, workable purpose.

PERSONAL MISSION STATEMENT for _____:

CHAPTER 4

The Magic Question

"Each problem has hidden in it an opportunity so powerful that it literally dwarfs the problem. The greatest success stories were created by people who recognized a problem and turned it into an opportunity." — Joseph Sugarman

As a senior leader, the biggest problem I see in business today among new MBA School graduates is that somehow, with the amazing and instantaneous access to information via the Internet, we have lost the art of critical thinking. Nor do school curriculums help in this matter. Teachers are working from programs designed at the turn of the last century. What has resulted is a business education system where professors do more "telling" than "asking" and students can Google anything versus actually thinking through a problem as part of the entire solution.

Recently, I had a discussion with a well-known nuclear fusion scientist; he told me his biggest problem is that the new Ph.D. graduates he hires have no ability for critical thinking.

When I first became a leader and had people reporting to me, I soon discovered that the people I was leading had problems—work-related and personal. Problems that they liked to dump on me! I used to think, "This isn't what I signed up for." After all, being a leader was supposed to be about going to high-powered meetings and doing "lunch," right?

Wrong!

People on my team had problems, and I thought that taking care of their issues was what leaders did. I then discovered that I was good at solving their problems. They would come into my office, sit down, dump their problems on my desk, and I would leap into action like some sort of steroid-charged superhero (minus the cape—although a cape would have been a nice touch). The problem dumpers would then happily stand up, spin around, and leave—dusting the symbolic dirt from their hands.

Word soon spread about my superhuman ability to take on all the worries of everyone in the company. Some days there seemed to be a line up outside my office. All that was missing was a "Take a Number" dispenser and magazines.

I found my days getting longer. I started coming in earlier and staying later—using off hours to do the paperwork and emails that were part of my job. I rationalized that this situation was the typical life of a leader. I justified it to my wife by saying, "This busy period is only temporary and it will get better." It didn't. Note: If you ever hear yourself saying that to one of your loved ones, then you are kidding yourself like I was.

Then my boss started to notice, and to my surprise, he was not happy about it at all. He even reprimanded me for not delivering results. I attempted to rationalize with him that I was delivering results, "Look at all the problems I am solving." He simply replied that I was doing everyone else's job, but they were paid to solve those problems. My job was to lead the team to deliver the results. He then left the room. He was like that. Give me shit and leave. Never did he give the new leader on the block any mentoring. Looking back on that now, I realize that made me stronger and a better leader by learning on my own what all great leaders know.

So I decided that was it! No more would I handle my people's problems. I took the chairs out of my office so others would not come in, sit down, and unload. Forever innovative, they started to bring their own chairs with them!

I decided not to comment on the problem they were attempting to dump on me. I would just sit there in silence and listen to them. I discovered that they then took the opportunity to dispatch more of their woes—occasionally even throwing in something from their personal lives. I realized the situation was not improving, and I wasn't happy about it.

The solution didn't come to me until I was at a strategy session with the senior team.

The facilitator was taking the group through a visioning exercise. She asked us to get into teams in front of different flip charts around the room. Then she instructed us that if there were no barriers at all in front of us, what would we do with the business? She threw out, "What would perfect look like?" As a young, newly minted manager, I watched my team members struggle with the question. It dawned on me that there was no such thing as "perfect," and the team could not fathom that state. So I simply said, "Guys, what would good look like?" Well, the flip chart pen started flying and pages were filled in rapid succession. I was amazed. I saw people's faces immediately change and ideas flowed effortlessly. Everyone could imagine the possibilities of "good" because it was achievable and realistic.

The magic question was born: "What would good look like?"

I soon started using the magic question in my daily life. When employees came into my office with their problem *de jour*, I would patiently listen and then ask them, "What does good look like to you?" They would always stop dead in their tracks, look thoughtfully skyward, and with released frustration and newfound enthusiasm, would start talking about potential solutions. They would leave my office, thanking me for the help, and most importantly, take their problems with them. It was remarkable!

Mind-boggling. My team members were more engaged. They got more done. The business moved further ahead. My boss was happier because results were improving. And all I did was stop solving people's problems by becoming more facilitative (fancy term for asking questions and not giving answers!).

I started using the magic question at home with my wife and kids. When my teenage daughter was venting her drama *de jour*, I would listen, wait for her to breathe, and then ask her, "What would good look like?" Same result. Instant change in body language and facial expression. Her thought process switched right away to solving the situation, and usually, with realistic resolutions.

I use it all the time now. In board meetings, with frontline employee groups, angry customers, when leading strategy sessions, when teaching, and in any situation where there is a conflict or problem that needs solving. In any situation where I want individuals or teams to envision something different or to tackle a mountain that has yet to be climbed.

Make the magic question part of your leadership arsenal. Prepare to be amazed!

In the space below, write down "What would good look like?" for a problem that you are facing right now in business or your personal life. Go crazy listing potential solutions. No limitations. Just ideas.

_____

_____

_____

_____

_____

_____

_____

_____

When could you have used the Magic Question at work today?

CHAPTER 5

Keep It Simple—A Lesson from NASA

"Simplicity is the ultimate sophistication."
— Leonardo da Vinci

The space pen—a high-tech ink pen for NASA. All sorts of myths and rumors exist about this fascinating pen developed in the 1960s as NASA geared up for its race to the moon against the Russians.

Just after President John F. Kennedy gave his amazing speech to Congress in May of 1961, the National Aeronautics and Space Administration (NASA) had a lot of engineering problems on its hands, not the least of which was, "How the heck are we going to do this?" At the time, NASA had barely put a program into place for sending a single man into orbit, let alone sending a crew all the way to the moon and safely back to earth. Talk about a "To Do" list!

One of the problems faced by the engineers was that they needed to develop a pen for the astronauts that could withstand freezing cold, desert heat, extremes in pressure, gravitational forces, and could write upside down and function in a zero gravity environment.

Rumor has it that NASA spent an enormous amount of money (perhaps as much as $12 billion) to develop this space pen. Truthfully, NASA only had a budget of $500 million for the entire project.

Ultimately, the astronauts ended up using a special nitrogen-pressurized pen called the "Fisher Space Pen," which was developed by Paul C. Fisher after thousands of hours of research and design and millions of dollars of his own money.

The Russians at the time used a…pencil—25 cents at the local drugstore.

This difference highlights the tendency among very intelligent and technical people to overcomplicate and overdo what could be solved by a very simple answer.

I see the same thing in business almost every day. Highly intelligent people will sit around for hours on end in meeting rooms to design complex solutions to simple problems, such as: complex I.T. solutions, CRM systems, accounting systems, long processes. However, most of these complex solutions are designed for the comfort and convenience of the company—not the customers.

One of the many hats a leader must wear is "Solution Facilitator." (A big booming, echoing voice should accompany that title!). The Solution Facilitator's job is to help the organization's members wrap their heads around potential solutions that are good for customers, good for employees, and good for the company. Key to the job is insuring they never allow complex, expensive solutions that require a Ph.D. to implement, use, and maintain. No offence to the Mensa IQ's out there, but simple is easier to understand and implement. Simple has a lower overall cost, higher customer satisfaction, and usually generates more revenue in the long run.

Members of the organization (maybe even your boss) may scoff at your approach as too simple. I have even suffered this wrath myself when a former boss (a Ph.D.) could not wrap his head around simple solutions because answers to problems "cannot be that easy!" This person turned out to be a leadership disaster because no one could or would follow him.

Believe me; you need to get good at simple. Get great at understanding what customers need and then find the easiest and fastest way to get it to them. While your competitors are over-engineering things, you will be out delivering and generating revenue.

By the way, the international astronauts of today still use the Fisher Space Pen. You can have one of your own by purchasing directly from the Fisher Space Pen Company for about fifty dollars. As for me, I'll stick with my pencil.

What process in your business might you be over-thinking?

How can you simplify it?

CHAPTER 6

Pit Stop—Teamwork that Drives Results

"Alone we can do so little; together, we can do so much."
— Helen Keller

I love watching Formula One race events. But it's not the actual race that hooks me into the action. Believe it or not, it's the pit stops!

In September 2005, I was fortunate to be invited to the Monza F1 in Milan where we were guests of Vodafone's CEO in the Paddock Club (a fantastic space directly above Pit Lane where our team's cars come in for their pit stops). It was a perfectly hot Italian Sunday afternoon. The food was first rate. Prior to the race, Ferrari's top pilot and the sport's all time winning driver, Michael Schumacher, came by the Paddock to talk to our group and answer questions. It was pretty heady stuff. One of those "lifestyles of the rich and famous" moments.

The crowd around the track was divided into camps, each supporting its favorite team—usually based on the nationality of the team's driver. It was a very special festive environment with national flags, colorful outfits, and singing everywhere.

When the race began, I settled into a great seat situated right at the finish line out on the deck of the Paddock Club. I watched the first few laps of the race. The cars flew by my position at over 300 kilometers (186 miles) per hour with the sound of a jet fighter plane. After a few minutes, I found it difficult to watch because they soared by with such blinding speed. It was impossible to tell which car was which and who was winning. Still the crowd loved it!

My view of the Renault pit

Soon, the first car pitted—the term racers use for when a car comes into their team's race side garage for fuel, tires, or mechanical adjustments. As the pit station for the Renault F1 Team was directly below where I was sitting, I had the best seat in the place to watch the action in the pit!

Pitting is the most important feature of any car race. Literally, millions of dollars are on the line each time a race is held. Because of the incredible speeds, a race is easily won or lost in the pits. When a car pits for a stop of 6-12 seconds, a competitor travelling at an average of 150 kilometers per hour can gain 400-800 meters, or a half-mile, on the leader.

Pit stops are crucial because they allow the car to carry less fuel—making them lighter and faster. They can run softer tires (which wear out faster) to enable better traction, thereby giving the driver more control at higher speeds. As well, the pit crew can make mechanical adjustments to the car for better handling in changing conditions.

Business leaders can learn a tremendous amount from every aspect of a pit stop. To begin with, a detailed strategic plan is developed for each and every race. The team looks at weather, lighting, the weight of fuel (it is different for diverse temperatures and altitudes), fuel consumption, track speed and condition (for tire wear), stopping distance, cornering speeds, what the other teams may be doing, etc. No strategic SWOT (Strength, Weakness, Opportunity, and Threat) is overlooked.

Next, the strategy is thoroughly shared with every team member. The entire team then goes to work rehearsing the new strategy (which includes spying on other teams to try figuring out another team's strategy for that race). It is not unusual for a pit team to practice five hours on a new strategy for a race—the equivalent of 3,000 six-second pit stops!

The team's strategy is carefully crafted and modeled so it knows and is comfortable with exactly how much "time" it is willing to "give away" to a competitor.

Strategies are also developed for unscheduled pit stops by drivers, such as changing weather, race cautions, and mechanical failures.

What I find amazing is that an F1 Pit Crew consists of over twenty members who take on individual and highly specialized roles for changing tires and carrying tires, including front and rear "jack men," firefighters, fuelers, fuel carriers, starters, and my favorite, the "lollipop man." The lollipop man is the air traffic controller for the whole operation. He stands in front of the car and holds out a long stick with a round sign on its end—it looks like a big lollipop, hence the name. Believe it or not, the sign reads on one side "Brakes On" and "First Gear" on the other side. You would think the driver—who is paid millions of dollars each season—would be smart enough to know he has to keep the brakes on when in the pit, and he needs to start out in first gear when it is time to go. However, forty years of pit stop accidents show that many a driver has eagerly stepped on the gas when his car was still attached to a fuel hose or tire jack!

The lollipop man is the pit boss. He is like the COO. Behind the actual pit box, he is managing information coming at him and the team from engineers back at the factory who are monitoring the car's performance data via satellite, from engineers sitting track-side who are monitoring hundreds of other data points, and from the drivers via radio communications. He then has to make decisions about what to do with the information, how it plays into the strategy, what his team can do and what the driver can do—all just to gain fractions of seconds on competitors….just like leaders need to do every day in business.

The rest of the pit crew operates like a finely tuned orchestra, making spectacular, albeit, fast music. They train as intensely as professional athletes—keeping up very demanding cardio and weight programs for peak fitness.

In a pit stop, an F1 car can scream into the pit, get 70 liters of fuel, four new tires, and have mechanical adjustments done; the driver gets water and his visor cleaned, and he is on his way again in six seconds. The lollipop man waits until the entire 20-24 team members have completed their individual tasks, and each one gives him the "done and safe" signal. The lollipop man has to take all that action in, make sure no other cars are coming, and release the driver back onto the track—talk about pressure and stress!

The team does all this for not only one car and driver but for two as F1 rules stipulate that each needs to have two cars in each race but only one pit crew! The team performs in unbearable temperatures while wearing full double-layer, fire retardant suits.

Yet, through all this chaos, each team member knows his role and responsibility. Not one team member is looking over the shoulder of the other guy, questioning his ability and competence. No one tries to do someone else's job. They just trust each other completely.

When the race is over and the winners are on the podium, the pit crew celebrates along with the driver. They know that only the driver can be on the podium. They are proud of their teammates and their driver. No one on the team says, "Oh, there he goes again! What a show-off!"

They know they may have a minor role and make a fraction of the money the driver makes, but they know the driver would not be there on the podium if it were not for the entire team. The driver knows it as well, and after he poses for the mandatory photo with some long-legged model, he rushes to the railing and tips his hat to his pit crew and then sprays them with a magnum of champagne and hands the trophy and the win over to the team!

Business leaders can have this kind of top level teamwork embedded in their culture by making sure that:

1. Everyone knows the vision, mission, and values of the company.
2. Everyone knows why he or she is in business and what he does better than any other competitor in serving their customers.
3. Everyone knows the strategies and how the strategies deliver the vision successfully.
4. Everyone from the front office to the mailroom knows his or her role, responsibility, and how doing his job correctly affects the rest of the team and the bottom line in the company.
5. Everyone in the company knows how the team is doing, what course corrections are needed, who is responsible for making corrections, and what is the next milestone.
6. Everyone knows that he or she cannot be on the podium, but that when a sales guy brings in a big order, the entire company wins and that each person played a key role in that win.
7. Celebration is a key part of the team's routine!

Do your business colleagues or team members spend time looking over each other's shoulders to see whether the others are doing their jobs?

Do you hear complaints around the table about other people and maybe even suggestions about other people's levels of competence?

How can you make your pit stop team players proud of their important roles in your business?

How are you going to change this behavior?

CHAPTER 7

Execute Like a Pilot—It's all about Vision, Structure, and Focus

"The successful warrior is the average man, with laser-like focus."
— Bruce Lee

Other than mothers, pilots are the finest multi-taskers there are. Pilots are also the finest executors of any professionals. As a leader, you and your career will go to heights (excuse the pun) unimaginable if you can learn and put into practice the secret that pilots use on every flight to get things done.

A pilot's level of training, consistency, and structure are what make the air the safest route to travel from one place to another. A pilot may have thousands of hours of flight time, and he or she may, even while blindfolded, know the precise location of every one of the hundreds of switches, knobs, levers, fuses, breakers, dials, and gauges found in a cockpit. Pilots know the feel of their aircrafts as if they are extensions of their own bodies. Pilots fly in the most brutal weather conditions—sometimes taking off and landing with next to zero visibility. Yet, they always, without fail, follow a strict procedure of pre-flight, pre-takeoff, climb, cruise, landing, and post-flight checklists. This routine keeps them on plan and focused.

When a pilot takes his very first flight as a student, he starts on that initial day with a message that is repeated to pilots over and over:

1. Fly ahead of the airplane.
2. If something goes wrong:
    a. Get the airplane under control.
    b. Find the nearest place to land.
    c. Land the plane.

"Fly ahead of the airplane" simply means always to be thinking one or two seconds ahead of what the aircraft will do. Planes, and even more so jets, take a little bit of time for the control input from the pilot to take effect in the aircraft. Always staying ahead of the airplane prevents any traumatic hard landings and close calls.

When something goes wrong, a pilot's training kicks in as if by instinct. Control the plane, find an airport, and land the plane. A pilot will never sit there and ponder the question, "I wonder what caused that? Let's get the manuals out to see whether we can discover the problem." That only happens when a bunch of managers get together in a boardroom.

The pilot's plan is: Land the airplane; figure out the cause later.

Pilots are known for focused and precise execution. Like a business, they have a destination. They have a plan for how they are going to get there.

A pilot knows that his aircraft is capable of the journey and he has enough resources—similar to a factory, a leader should know whether the operation is capable of the journey and whether the available resources are qualified for the job.

Pilots have governance for the execution of the plan in the form of checklists, and they have waypoints along the journey to track progress. Similarly, leaders should always be checking progress to plan.

In an aircraft operation, clear and precise communications are given to other flight crew personnel on board and to the ground controllers and company and vice versa. In business, companies with a solid record for successful execution have always had clear communications rooted in the attainment of their goals. Every stakeholder—from leaders, to the board, partners, vendors, unions, and every single member of the company's frontline team—knows exactly what his or her role and responsibility is. The guy taking out the garbage from the kitchen in a hotel restaurant knows exactly how his performance affects the chef's ability to get meals out on time and to meet the customer's standards. He knows how not doing his job correctly and on time impacts revenue, productivity, costs, and customer satisfaction.

I have heard managers tell me that pilots have a very narrow job focus, and they don't have the day-to-day issues that management faces in business. (Notice how I said "managers" and not "leaders"? That's because managers usually come up with reasons why things cannot be done, versus leaders who find a way to make things happen). Aircrews work in an environment that is very complex, dynamic, and features multiple things going on at one time. Not only do they have to worry about the safety, comfort, and convenience of their crew and passengers, but they have to monitor and manage the weather, air traffic control instructions, weights and balances, fuel systems and fuel flow, hydraulic systems, electrical systems, navigation, communication and radar systems, multiple engines, altitude, auto-pilot systems, cabin pressure and temperature, and the list goes on.

Yet with all this to monitor, air crews stick to their plans and focus purely on execution. If something goes wrong, their single-minded focus is: "Fly the aircraft and land at the nearest safe location." That's it; that's all.

Successful leaders also know that execution is elusive in most organizations. In fact, 97 percent of all leaders who have a strategic plan will fail to execute their plan because of their lack of leadership based on some very basic principles. After the executives have gone off to the mountains for a three-day strategy retreat where they drink some good wine and develop the new plan, they return to the office very excited, stating, "This time it is going to be different!" Then most return to the same old ways of mediocre performance. So what's missing?

The 3 percent of companies that execute know this: For a plan to be implemented successfully, the senior leaders have to take an active role. They have to detail and communicate the plan to each and every stakeholder in the business. They have to ensure that every single person on the team understands his or her individual roles, responsibilities, and how doing his job affects the company's success. People have to know how they are going to be measured. The senior leaders then need to implement a regular program of governance where, at least monthly, the plan is reviewed to ensure that the implementation is on track. If the team is off plan, the executives need to understand why and implement course corrections. Re-communicating every month to the team is critical. Just as a pilot checks in and communicates at regular checkpoints, an organization's team needs to know how it is doing. This is a huge motivator!

Unsuccessful businesses mainly suffer from the same infection. Senior leaders think they are the only ones who know what is going on and that regular frontline employees would not understand, so it's best if we just keep driving them on metrics they do not know or buy into. I call it "corporate archery"— it's what happens when you give a person a bow and arrow, blindfold him, and expect the archer to hit a bull's eye. The best leaders in the world, like pilots, follow a very structured approach to strategy, implementation, and communication to the entire team. Interesting as well, these organizations have the highest levels of employee engagement, customer satisfaction, and profitability. Coincidence?

Regardless of whether you are leader of one or many, do you have a process established to document action plans and a calendar follow-up to insure that projects are on track?

Do you regularly review action plans for strategies or projects to make sure things are on budget and on time?

Does everyone know what his or her roles and responsibilities are for each action?

Can all actions be measured?

Does everyone know what the score is—that is, do they know what results have been achieved?

CHAPTER 8

Get Your Car Keys—Solution Finder vs. Problem Finder

"Impossible only means that you haven't found the solution yet."
— Jim Rohn

In the following story, I put into action some advice I originally heard from business great Peter Legge. At that time, in 1998, I was leading a $200 million desktop lifecycle business (Desktop Lifecycle services are all about completely owning the customer's I.T. infrastructure environment and charging a simple recurring operating expense each month while lifting the I.T. expense off the customer's balance sheets).

It was the beginning of the new fiscal year, so I was rolling out the new targets for the team to achieve. We had just come off a fantastic growth year, and our expectations were to do much the same level of business during the coming twelve months.

I had the team together in a meeting room. I put up on a screen a slide showing the revenue forecast that needed to be delivered for the coming year. Well, you would have thought that I had asked people to rock by rock disassemble Mount Everest, move the pieces to Antarctica, and reassemble it rock by rock. The moans and groans! The excuses! "There is not enough market out there to support that kind of revenue. We don't have enough resources. That's too hard in this economy. We pulled out all the growth opportunities last year. Customers are getting too cost conscious. The competition is charging way less than we are. Inflation is too high…" The complaining went on and on. Despite my reasoning that the research had been done and the target was very achievable, no one was listening.

Finally, after about fifteen minutes, I calmly interrupted and said, "Go get your car keys and meet me in the parking lot in five minutes." I packed up my meeting material and left the room.

Even though what I was about to do was pushing the edge of leadership sanity, my team members needed a shake-up in their thinking. I went to my office, grabbed my jacket and car keys, and walked out to the parking lot.

Minutes later, the entire team had assembled in the parking lot. Still looking dazed and confused, they stood around my car and continued with the questions and complaining. I stuck my head out the car window, said, "Get in your cars and follow me," and drove away.

I drove very slowly out of the parking lot—constantly checking my rearview mirror to see whether they would follow. They were dutifully, albeit reluctantly, falling into formation behind me. Out on the street, I led a procession of ten cars on a journey of left and right turns and right and left turns. We winded our way through commercial areas and residential streets. All along, I kept checking my mirror and controlling my speed so everyone could keep up. Like a mother duck leading her newborn babies to water, we wandered through the community for about twenty minutes.

Once I was completely satisfied that the team was thoroughly frustrated with the seemingly pointless journey, we arrived at the Royal Oak Cemetery. I stopped my car, got out, and started to walk into the cemetery. I casually checked over my shoulder to see whether they were still following me. They were. About 100 meters into the pristine park-like setting, I stopped on a hill overlooking most of the expansive cemetery. It was a beautiful winter morning in Vancouver. The sun was shining. A light fog hung over the cemetery's lower end. It was surprisingly warm for January. One-by-one, the team strolled up beside me. When the last one arrived, an irritated and outspoken team member blurted out, "Okay, Bob, what is this all about?" I raised my hand in front of me and slowly let it roll across the landscape of headstones. Then I replied, with almost a whisper, "You see all those people out there? Every one of them would gladly change places with you in an instant. Do you think we could focus on what a great team we have? On how we have an amazing product, solid financial backing, a very loyal customer base, and figure out how we are going to make it work this year to the best of our ability?"

You could have heard a pin drop onto the dew covered grass. Reality hit home for each and every one of them. Most of us, including you reading this book, have it really good. We have a great life. A home to go to. Food in the refrigerator. Family and friends who love us dearly and cannot imagine life without us. The beauty of life for most of us is that we have the ability to choose to be the very best at what we do. Or, we can choose to wallow in self-pity and focus on why things will not work versus using our unlimited brain-power to make them happen.

After a few minutes of quiet reflection, I turned and walked back to my car. Every one silently followed. When I arrived back at the office, I went into the meeting room where we had started that morning. Within minutes, everyone had joined me. Some thanked me. It was like a brand new day. Charged with a fresh outlook and new energy, we got down to the task of planning how we were going to achieve our target without even a hint of negativity.

People in general will usually take the path of least resistance. It is in our DNA to save time and energy. Sometimes, that comes out in the form of pushback and negative energy. It is a leader's job, however, to see that and push through it, building compelling visions for the organization to follow—to inspire them to go where they would not normally go on their own. Sometimes, a leader really has to push the boundaries to show everyone on the team just how capable he or she really is.

That year, we achieved 160 percent of the forecasted target we were given.

What would you have done differently to bring the team to solution focus?

How do you respond to seemingly impossible challenges that are put in front of you?

CHAPTER 9

What Are You Famous For?—Providing Value Starts with Knowing What Value You Provide

"You do not merely want to be considered just the best of the best. You want to be considered the only ones who do what you do."
— Jerry Garcia, Ben and Jerry's Ice Cream

The world's greatest organizations—the ones that have happy employees, satisfied customers, and a growing bottom line—all share a common trait. They all know what they are famous for. They know why customers buy from them. They know what they need to focus on in order to continue growing. They have a clear focus on being innovators, driving quality, operational efficiency, and customer intimacy, but they never try to be all things to all people. The world's great organizations have laser beam focus on being great at one thing and getting good at other areas.

Apple is great at being an innovative company; it's probably the most famous innovator of recent times. Four Seasons Hotels and Nordstrom's are world leaders in customer intimacy. Wal-Mart, Costco, and McDonald's are famous for their consistency and good prices because of their intense focus on operational efficiency. GE is single-minded in its approach to quality—leading the world with its Six Sigma excellence.

The key is that it's all about focus—focus on a greatness that gets the entire organization pulling in the same direction and climbing the same mountain.

Companies that are great at customer experience, like WestJet or Southwest Airlines, with their "Fun and Friendly" approach, are also very good at landing an airplane, unloading, loading it up again, and taking off faster than their competitors. Still, their key strategic focus is the customer's experience.

Costco is known for great prices. It also has a very good return policy for defective products, but Costco's key strategic focus is on low prices.

The same is true for individual leaders. Their strengths are what got them to where they are today. If you are a leader, you are famous for what got you the leadership job and any promotions, not for your weaknesses.

You may have been hired because you fulfilled a need the company had for a professional engineer, an MBA, or a chartered accountant. But now that you have the job, what have you done to establish yourself as the very best there is at what you do?

Today, I arrive on the job far differently from when I started out some thirty years ago. My strengths have evolved into a leadership role, and in fact, it is because I am a good leader that I have been hired for various executive roles over the last fifteen years. I started as a marketer and I was very good at what I did. I was recognized for innovation in my creativity with three very prestigious marketing awards. I realized, however, that as a marketer, even with the fancy glass awards that adorned the cabinet, I needed skills that would make me more valuable at a strategic level. The answer was to become world-class at leadership.

I began to study other leaders—past and present, good and bad. I found mentors. I turned my car into a university on wheels with countless audio books on leadership by some of the best leaders and business gurus in the world like Peters, Drucker, Waitley, Iacocca, and Welch. I read every book I could get my hands on. School was never out for me on the subject of leadership and strategy. Today, my classroom is composed of e-Books on my iPad, YouTube, blogs, and Internet sites like www.ted.com.

My key point here is: I have known lots of functional experts in marketing, finance, and operations who were amazing at their jobs. Some had awards like myself for the jobs they performed. Today, some are still in functional roles, but most have been outsourced, downsized, or put out to early retirement. Managers do not have a shelf-life. Only leaders do. Those who get good at leadership find increasingly senior roles and find it easier to break into new companies and new industries.

As I said at the beginning of this chapter, when you break into a management role, you need to work hard to become world-class at it. Become the very best accountant there is. Be renowned for your abilities to run a logistics centre. Whatever it is, be the very best! Turn your education into leadership. Get good at leading people into change. Use your drive to become the world's best at it. Become known as the guy (or girl) who can get an engaged team of people to achieve amazing results in the face of hopeless odds.

Don't have people reporting to you? Get good at being a leader anyway! Be the person who knows the business' strategy inside and out. Look for every opportunity you can find to present ideas to senior management. Find an internal sponsor who is senior to you, tell him or her what you want to do, and ask for advice on becoming the company's next leader. Show your leadership by being the absolute best there is at your job. And, while you are waiting for your moment to step onto the leadership stage, learn as much as you can about every aspect of leading.

Be famous in your network for what you do. Then become famous for leading others.

What are you good at in your business that you can do even better so you become famous for it?

If you were the absolute best in the world at what you do, what would you need to do to be recognized as such?

CHAPTER 10

Lessons from Billy Idol

"It is truly said: It does not take much strength to do things, but it requires great strength to decide what to do." — Chow Ching

In August, 2002, I was the vice president of a large Canadian telephone company. I had been brought in about three months previously to do a turn-around on the business. At the time, the business had twenty operating call centres in Western Canada with 1,500 employees. The turn-around was required because some key business metrics were way out of whack. Namely, the company had the industry's worst customer satisfaction, the worst cost per call, and a wide-ranging level of engagement to apathy among its front-line team. And, the general feeling among people both inside and out of the business was that there would be no change.

The company president asked me to turn-around the business or find a way to divest and give the company's customers better service from an outsourcer. Right up my alley—I love turning around businesses!

Just as I got into the turn-around, the mother ship got into some trouble on the markets. The stock price fell from just over $60 to almost $5. Analysts were concerned about the amount of debt the organization was carrying— debt that had been incurred to build out the network in anticipation of major dot.com generated data traffic. Because the dot.com market had fallen apart in 2000 and 2001, now there was a vastly underutilized network and massive debt. To top it off, the Moody's Debt rating for the company had been significantly lowered. Analysts wanted to see a big jump in EBITDA (Earnings Before Interest, Depreciation, and Amortization) in order to recommend the stock as a "Buy."

The president gathered the troops on a massive leadership conference call and quite simply said, "Find a way to reduce your operating budgets in the next three months by 30 percent. End of discussion."

An executive has few options to raise profitability. Generating more revenue takes time. Increasing productivity takes time too. Lowering costs is one of the few levers a business leader can pull for quick results. I was already implementing a major turn-around project. To reduce further my cost in a business where employees are your only assets, I had only one tool in the kit: repurposing or laying-off part of my team.

After running the numbers and models, I realized 30 percent of the staff— 500 people—would need to be let go, and I would have to close nine locations while consolidating a couple of others. I would have to continue to drive customer satisfaction improvements and employee engagement. I would have to install an automated system of some sort to handle the front end of a customer call, and I would need to distribute the workload to the agents taking calls.

All the previous business turn-arounds I had done were accomplished through a growth model. For the first time, I had to grow and improve the overall business by letting go of a third of my workforce. Privately, few words could be used to describe the situation other than "Holy crap!"

This whole process would be an amazing business study for any MBA class. But I wasn't just studying it—I was living it!

My leadership style is to lead with vision, focus the team intensely on outcomes, and do it while being highly visible and accessible. My belief is that if there is ugly work to be done, then I am going to be in the trenches leading it. And that is where we started. We pulled in all the managers to one location (almost a hundred of them) and clearly communicated the problem and the proposed solution. Some managers in the room received the message that their operations were going to grow; other managers heard that their offices were soon going to close. Highly emotional stuff!

I was amazed that, through clear, open, and honest communication, including what everyone's roles and responsibilities were, the management team was able to pull together and lead the mission. They were the most courageous people I have ever worked with. A real inspiration!

To become highly visible, we came up with a communication plan that had me going into each operation about to be shut down as quickly as possible so I would be available to all the employees to answer their questions: Why them? Why their office? What did this mean to them at the individual level?

It was quite an experience—one I will never forget because it was so emotionally charged. I was going into deeply depressed economic regions where the jobs were the best in the town and many of the employees were the sole breadwinners for their families. So many tears. So many angry people. My heart really went out to everyone.

I started to receive death threats, and many times, I could swear I was being followed. The company got me a security detail, but that only made me feel the pressure all the more. My daily start-up routine now included a security briefing and reviews of plans to "egress the package" (aka me) in case something went down.

I had a panic button on a pager type device on my belt. If something were "starting to go down," the two security guys would get me out of the building and into a car per a planned exit route. At one meeting with employees at a highly militant affected closure office, a female employee was very upset and blamed me for potentially putting her family on the street and forcing them to steal for their living. She then paused and looked me straight in the eye and said, "I have a gun, you know." I panicked! I pushed the button. The door burst open and my two burly shadows had me in their arms, down some stairs, around a corner, and into a car faster than the rush at a Black Friday sale.

I was a wreck.

But still, I kept it quiet from my family and my team. They all needed to see strength, confidence, and purpose. The "Road Show" had to go on. I was committed to being in every city as quickly as possible to face the music and foster the change process.

At the beginning of August 2002, I was in Kelowna, British Columbia to meet with some forty-nine employees who were about to lose their jobs. The hotel where we were staying was close to the lake and an amazing running trail. That morning, I decided to ditch the security team and go for a run on my own to clear my head.

It was an amazing summer morning—so peaceful and spectacularly beautiful. I was just outside the hotel, bent over to tie my shoes, when I heard this British voice behind me ask, "You going for a run?" As I stood up and started to turn around to reply, "Yes, I…" I stopped in mid-sentence. This guy standing in front of me was dressed in running gear head-to-toe, had tattoos on his forearms, was about 5' 10", skinny but fit, had bleached blond, spiky hair, and blue-tinted sunglasses. He looked exactly like Billy Idol—the rock star! I finished my sentence by repeating, "Yes, I am." He then asked, "Mind if I run with you?" Still completely dumbfounded, I replied, "Ya, sure."

Off we went to the trail along the lake. All I could think about was how much this guy looked like Billy Idol. I was so stunned that I didn't even introduce myself or ask him his name. I just kept telling myself that he could not be Billy Idol because rock stars do not run at 7 o'clock in the morning—they are just getting to bed at 7 o'clock in the morning—and certainly, rock stars do not run with guys like me. It must be one of those weird coincidences. After all, everyone in the world has a twin somewhere, right?

As we are running along, I note that the Billy Idol look-alike is in pretty good shape and has no problem doing an eight-minute pace. I continue to reason with myself that rock stars aren't in shape to run that fast. He asks me what I do. I reply that I am an executive with the local phone company. I ask him what he does; he replies that he is a musician. Freaky, right? Not only does he look like Billy Idol, but he's a musician as well. Maybe he's one of those impersonators. A rock star wouldn't be up at this time of the morning, wouldn't be running, and certainly wouldn't be in Kelowna of all places.

He then asks me what I'm doing in Kelowna. So I unfold the whole sad story of my current situation and the grief I am inflicting on the people affected by the downsizing. He listens. When I pause for air, he says, "What about the rest of people in the business who are going to be staying? How are they feeling about all of this? They are the ones moving the business forward afterwards; how are you keeping them motivated? They have to be going through some kind of guilt and worry."

"Trout mouth" was the only way to describe me! Trout mouth is when someone is so flabbergasted, confused, and stunned, that he looks like a fish suspended in the water with its mouth gaping open. I was so fixated on the part of the business that was winding down that I had completely forgot the part of the business that was going to be turned around and become the industry benchmark for engagement, service, and profitability.

My mind started to spin. We kept running along. By now, we were headed back to the hotel. My consultant/leadership/advisor/running partner and I finished up our run, exchanged sweaty handshakes, and wished each other a great day. When we parted, I still did not know his name.

Confusion, frustration, and opportunity washed over me as I shaved and showered for the day. Who was this guy? How could he see something so obvious that was missing in my leadership?

Because of him, I shifted part of my focus to the employees remaining. They had to be fearful that they were next. They had to be suffering from a little bit of survivor's guilt, a natural reaction in the change process.

I got dressed, grabbed my stuff, and headed downstairs for breakfast with my team, which consisted of a couple of pissed off security guards (because I had gone running without them) and my communications manager, who was assisting me in delivering the message on the tour.

After getting an earful from the security detail, I told them about the run I had just had. When I got to the part about this guy looking like Billy Idol, my communications manager sat straight up, and with the look of someone bursting with news to share, yelled out, "Billy Idol is staying at this hotel! He is playing in town tonight!"

Trout mouth again. I couldn't even speak—which according to my wife, never happens. Not only had I run for forty-five minutes with Billy Idol, but he had given me some "between the eyes" advice that I would have been charged $10,000 for by some consultant.

We completed the task ahead. The day was filled with more people yelling at me, more tears, more frustration from employees about to lose their livelihoods, interspersed with the odd person who came up to me, shook my hand, and expressed appreciation for not hiding in my office but coming to talk to them in person.

On the four-hour drive home to Vancouver that night, we talked about a plan to engage the 1,000 people who would be left. How would we get them focused on the vision, the mission, and the strategies? How would their individual roles and responsibilities lift the business to one that was going to thrive, grow, and become a key contributor to the company's overall success?

Leadership is all about getting people to do things willingly that they would not normally do on their own. It's about being there front and centre to take away people's fears, to help people achieve their dreams, while at the same time, fulfilling your vision through the team. Painting clear pictures of what good looks like, and letting the team know that during the climb ahead, there will be challenges, problems, and roadblocks. Inspiring them to see through the obstacles and create solutions.

A leader truly does get people to dance to music that has yet to be written.

On any particular day, your job as a leader will have you being a coach, a councilor, a priest, a teacher, a mom, a friend, an autocrat, a social director, an air traffic controller, an orchestra conductor, a mentor, and a cheerleader. You have to groove with ambiguity, and at the same time, be crystal clear and resolute in your focus on the vision and direction of the business.

People will not always like your decisions or what you have to say; however, they will respect you for it when they know why and how they play a role in the plan. Every human on the planet wants to do a good job and be valued for his or her contribution. Your job as a leader is to ensure that your entire team—or if you don't have a team, those around you—discovers the way that everyone is able to deliver the most value he has to give.

Two postscripts to this story:

First, one year after doing the significant cost and employee cutting program, the business was recognized as having the lowest cost per call in the industry, the highest customer satisfaction, and the highest employee engagement in the company.

Second, Billy Idol, if you are reading this book somewhere, I owe you a beer.

What would you do in the same situation?

How could it have been handled differently?

Have you got a very tough change project in front of you right now?

What from the previous chapters in this book can you use to develop a world-class change plan?

CHAPTER 11

Doug—July 23rd, 1999

"It's not about you. It's about them." — *Clint Eastwood*

A leader learns plenty in business school about most matters of the head. But on the street, a leader learns lessons that connect the head to the heart and sometimes to the very soul.

Seldom do leadership lessons come more profound than the one I'm about to share. This lesson literally started on the street. And...it is the most painful chapter in this book for me to write.

In 1999, I was the general manager of a $200 million mix of businesses owned by BC Tel. I was leading a completely diversified group that had remote connections to the mother ship's core business. The businesses were a collection of concepts and services intended to complement the needs of the customers whom the main business served. The fact that the menagerie was under my leadership meant that the organizations were either in start-up mode or in need of a turn-around.

I was an anomaly within the company, so it was not always clear where my group should be residing. Consequently, I was placed within a larger group called Communications Systems. This group was headed by my mentor, leadership advisor, and good friend, Kevin Heaney. Kevin is one of the finest leaders I have ever worked under, with, and around. His ability to get people to deliver amazing results with limited resources is beyond comparison. And, most importantly, he gets them to have more fun while delivering results than is probably allowed at most businesses in the world. Hard work and fun go hand-in-hand with Kevin. Kevin loves life and everything about it with kid-like enthusiasm! Oh, and did I mention that his education only went through the eleventh grade? Kevin is proof positive that leadership is far more than what gets taught at top business schools around the world.

Kevin is a huge believer in achieving success in business by insuring that happy employees are making sure that customers are satisfied. Part of creating a culture with happy employees is maintaining high visibility with the organization's leaders and openly sharing vision, mission, values, strategies, and goals as well as tough challenges that the team and the business need to overcome.

To accomplish this mission, the executive team regularly travelled together to all the company's operating regions to hold sessions with every employee to share this information. On July 23rd, 1999, we were in Calgary to meet 150 employees first thing on that Friday morning. Most of the Calgary team was made up of the I.T. and Technical Operations side of our business and was headed up by Doug Erickson, our C.T.O.

Doug was fifty-seven years old at the time while Kevin and I were both in our early forties. We affectionately called Doug "Dad" because of the worldly advice he always had for us; plus, he always kept a close eye on Kevin and me because we were always playing practical jokes on each other.

Kevin, Doug, and I were from Vancouver while the rest of our Executive Team was from Edmonton and Calgary. The three of us were staying at Calgary's landmark hotel, the Fairmont Palliser, a short three blocks from where the meeting was that day.

After an amazing meal the evening before, highlighted with great wine, we woke up to a gorgeous, cloudless summer day in Calgary. We ate an uneventful breakfast and headed out the door for the short walk to the meeting.

Just outside the hotel was a newspaper box; the day's paper featured an amazing full color picture (U.S. Navy Photo by Ensign John Gay, U.S. Navy, July 7th, 1999) of a F18 Hornet fighter jet against a clear blue sky and a peculiar circular cloud of fog around the mid-section of the fuselage. A remarkable picture because the photographer had captured the precise moment when the jet penetrated the sound barrier—the puff of cloud quickly formed and then disappeared in the blink of an eye.

U.S. Navy F/A 18 Hornet Bursting Through the Sound Barrier

Doug was a former radio service technician in the Canadian Air Force, and since I was a pilot, we immediately started talking about what a cool picture it was and how hard it must have been to capture it. Kevin wasn't saying much but was probably thinking, "What a couple of nerds!"

We continued talking about planes as we walked along. Kevin, becoming bored with our airplane discussion, started to pull away from us.

Just as we arrived at the building that housed our offices, Doug stopped in his tracks and just stood there. I looked at Doug and said, "What's up, Doug?" He replied, "I'm feeling a little dizzy." I said, "No problem. We're early. Let's just rest here a bit."

As I was replying to Doug, he started to fall toward the sidewalk. I lunged just in time to catch his head before it hit the concrete. In a second, I was down on my knees, cradling Doug's head in my lap. The skin on his face was clammy and turning blue. Kevin, who had already gone inside the building to the security desk, came back outside. Seeing the two of us down on the sidewalk, he yelled, "What happened?" Before he could finish speaking, I shouted, "Get an ambulance!" Kevin disappeared back inside; then, he was instantly back and down at my side. Without even saying a word to each other, we gently placed Doug on the sidewalk and assumed positions for doing CPR. No discussion. It was weird. Kevin took up position to apply chest compression, and I tilted Doug's head back, opened his mouth, and calmly reached inside it to remove his false teeth. Kevin looked at me and said, "Who knew?" (referring to Doug's false teeth).

Afterwards, I thought about how weird it was to have such instinctual communication with someone that we could just assume our roles and positions. No discussion. Just execution.

Kevin started chest compressions and counting out loud. When he got to five, it was my turn to give Doug a breath of my air. As I did, Kevin kept compressions going as he counted out loud. I got a blast of Doug's air back into my mouth and lungs from the force of Kevin on Doug's chest. I lost it temporarily and screamed at Kevin to stop when I was trying to give Doug air. Kevin simply said, "Sorry" and we carried on. At that moment, I became aware of a nameless, faceless woman kneeling beside me and softly saying, "It's okay; you are doing great. That's it. Good job."

Time slowed down. I became hyper-conscious of everything going on around us. The crowd forming. The traffic on the street. The smell of exhaust. Our executive colleagues had shown up and were silently clearing our suitcases and briefcases out of the way.

In between breaths, I yelled out, "Where's the ambulance?" The angelic coach beside me replied, "Don't worry; they are coming. Keep going." And as she said that, I could hear the sirens in the distance.

It seemed like an eternity!

A police cruiser arrived; the officer started asking our colleagues questions and taking notes.

Finally, the paramedics rolled up to the sidewalk and time started to speed up again. Four paramedics and firemen were rushing around with plastic boxes and oxygen tanks. Two came over to Kevin and me and very calmly informed us we were taking over. They thanked us as Kevin and I quietly stood up and stepped back. The police officer came over and started asking us who we were, what happened, blah, blah, blah. A paramedic asked us whether Doug was taking any medications. We replied that we did not know, but we could open his bag and check. He asked us to do that.

While we were opening and frantically searching through Doug's bag, I saw from the corner of my eye the paramedics cut off Doug's shirt, apply electrodes and wires to his chest, take his blood pressure, and administer oxygen. Then it got Hollywood and scary all at the same time. Out came the defibrillator paddles, and just like in the movies, the paramedic applying the paddles yelled out, "Clear!" He pushed the button and Doug's body jolted rigid.

It was completely surreal!

Another jolt of electricity. And another.

Then a long hypodermic needle with adrenalin was shot into Doug's chest. Another jolt of electricity.

The paramedics quickly gathered Doug onto a stretcher and into the back of the ambulance. Then off they went with full lights and sirens—leaving behind scattered piles of Doug's clothing, used up medical supplies, and wrappers. I looked around and the woman who I thought I had coaching me, was nowhere to be seen. The police officer directed Kevin and me into the backseat of his police cruiser and off we went with lights and sirens too.

The police car accelerated through the downtown morning rush hour traffic and quickly shot ahead of the ambulance and raced ahead. At every intersection, the police officer would stop in the middle of the intersection until the ambulance blasted by. Then he would repeat the procedure by racing ahead to the next intersection.

Within five minutes, we arrived at Foot Hills Hospital in Calgary. The police officer took us inside where we were met by a couple of nurses who started asking Kevin and me questions about Doug? His age? Was he taking medications? Question after question, most of which we could not answer. Funny how you can work closely with people for a few years and think you know them, but in reality....

The nurses asked us to sit in the waiting room and they disappeared. For the first time since this event had started to unfold, Kevin and I were alone. We just sat there and stared into the floor. Not a word was spoken.

About five minutes later, a nurse came and asked us to follow her. Without a word, we got up and dutifully followed. She took us to a small room with a couple of chairs, some nice paintings on the wall, and a Bible on the table. She asked us to wait there; someone would be coming to talk with us about Doug's condition.

I looked over to Kevin and said, "Nothing good ever comes in little rooms like this." With that, the door opened and a doctor stepped in and closed the door. He sat down and told us that Doug had not made it. Most likely, Doug had died of a massive coronary; there was absolutely nothing anyone could have done to save him. The doctor informed us that Doug would be sent down for an autopsy, and they would contact the family as soon as Doug's body could be claimed. With that, he shook our hands and left.

I was in shock. Kevin too. We just numbly got up and walked out into the morning sunshine. Kevin hailed a taxi and we both climbed inside to ride back to the office.

At that moment, the reality of it all hit me and tears started to well up in my eyes. Kevin, seeing this, looked over at me and said, "Who do you think we should get to replace him?"

I lost it! I started to yell at Kevin that Doug had just died! He was our friend! How could he be so cold! (I actually think I used the "F" word a lot during my tirade.)

Kevin let me vent, and then calmly, he said, "Look, Bob, you are a leader. Leaders think about their people first. And right now, we have back at the office 150 people and our executive colleagues who all know something happened, but they need to know what. They need to hear it from the two of us because we were with Doug. They need to know that we are leading this organization; otherwise, they will fall into despair about what this all means to them and their lives. We will deliver that message with the resolve of strong leaders who have it together. We will then communicate what happened to his wife, followed by the other offices over the phone. We will then start to dig into what Doug was working on so no one in the business takes on that burden as they grieve. We will then get on an airplane, fly home, and go meet with his wife and family and tell them what happened—that Doug was in no pain and that we were with him right to the end. Then, when you go home tonight, you have all weekend to grieve yourself because on Monday, you need to be back as a strong leader to support the team through this."

It was like being hit with a bucket of ice-cold water. But…Kevin was absolutely right. Then, still in the back of the taxi, and with the same wordless communication that we had when assuming CPR roles, we got our phones out and started making calls.

In the office, we communicated with our co-workers, explaining what had happened, and what would happen now. We talked about what a great leader Doug had been and how passionate he was about everything he did. We reminded the team that Doug would want us to keep on plan and do the cool things he knew we were going to do. That meeting was the second hardest thing I have ever had to do as a leader. (The first, in terms of toughest things I have had to do as a leader, was about to come later that day when Kevin and I were back in Vancouver and sitting in Doug's living room talking to his wife and son). I knew Kevin had been absolutely right as I witnessed the team come together. Hugs and tears were everywhere. Some came up to thank us for the message and empathized with us for the task we had. Some asked what they could do to help. Their grieving process had started.

Back in the home office in Vancouver, we put a call into Patricia Jecks, the marketing manager for my group. PJ, as I call her, was also a long-time colleague of Doug. He too was like a father to her. When I told PJ what had happened, she was devastated! We had about 100 people in the Vancouver office—all of them close to Doug. I asked PJ to take on her toughest leadership task to date. I asked her to assemble the team and inform them about Doug and…to do it with strength, compassion, and…to let everyone know how they could help. While we were cleaning up in Calgary and preparing to fly home, PJ was a rock star! The team members there were equally devastated; however, they too rose to the challenge with amazing strength.

We got people involved in moving forward. People back home went through files. We all got together and planned next steps. We named a meeting room after Doug and framed a copy of the F18 photo Doug and I had been talking about just before he died. The leadership brought the company tighter together.

I learned more about leadership that day than I could have found in any book or classroom. The entire organization over the next few weeks would become closer than ever before. Team members took on roles and tasks far outside their responsibilities. We celebrated Doug, his life, and his great contributions to our lives. We had an amazing year that year, and all along, we all did it for Doug.

Leaders have an amazing job! I love being a leader. That day in July 1999, I learned forever that leadership and life can never be taken for granted.

Leaders who truly know the power they hold never have to use their position power. True leaders who do not have position power have figured out how to make things happen in their organizations. They are leaders people will follow. People follow authentic leaders anywhere and do things they would not normally do on their own. Genuine leaders are rare because they have learned how to nurture the innate leadership skills they have onboard.

Are you the type of leader who is authentic so people want to follow you because they want to be part of something bigger and cooler? Or are you a fake leader, the type who needs to use a big stick constantly to move the ball down the field?

Authentic leaders put their team first and their personal agendas last. They know "what's in it for the team members" and they communicate that as part of their vision. Followers easily resonate with that message. Real leaders know that every day is about being a change agent. They do not fear change, and they work hard to ensure their team understands why change is happening and how it affects them. Followers have an easier time with change when they are informed and when they feel they can contribute to being part of the change.

Finally, the very best leaders in the world figure out how to bring balance into their lives; they live, laugh, and love for today, but they plan for tomorrow.

I learned on the street that day that you are alive and you are dead; it's that fast.

From the moment Doug, Kevin, and I left the hotel until Kevin and I were hailing a taxi after the hospital, the entire event took fifty minutes.

Some day will be your last. What are you doing in the meantime to leave a legacy that will make your friends and family proud?

CHAPTER 12

Running with Grizzly Bears

"Beware, so long as you live, of judging men by their outward appearance." — Jean de La Fontaine

In July of 2000, our executive team went on its annual strategic renewal retreat. For most organizations, the "Annual Strategy Retreat" is a bit of an inside joke among company non-executives  because the executives always go away into the mountains, eat, drink, and "high-five" each other for a couple of days, and with the help of a high-priced facilitator, develop a business changing strategy that will (they promise) change the company in amazing ways! For 97 percent of companies, however, nothing ever changes.

But our team was the 3 percent that made lasting changes because of what we decided on away from the office. That, however, is not what this chapter is about.

Our team decided on a quaint little riverside hotel in Canmore, Alberta. Canmore is a picturesque town set high in the Canadian Rockies and known worldwide for its outstanding golf, skiing, and hiking. Many of the world's elite athletes train in Canmore: cross-country skiers for its high altitude and mountain climbers for its tough, technical climbs.

Canmore is also known for its wildlife.

I am a runner. Running soothes my soul. I have run for nearly forty years because of the almost meditative state I am able to get into while out running and the solutions to tough problems I come up with while pounding the pavement or ripping up a trail. For me, running is not a chore—it is pure pleasure.

Upon waking on our first day in Canmore, I pulled on my shorts, shirt, laced up my runners, and headed down to the lobby with a plan to get out and enjoy the amazing trails along the river. Clean, fresh mountain air awaited my lungs. The peaceful tranquility of the river nestled among the trees in the valley would be the perfect environment for me to "zone-out." Or so I thought.

As I was heading out the door, the guy behind the reception desk yelled out, "You going for a jog?" (Oh, how runners hate the "jog" word!). I replied very energetically, "Absolutely!" He replied, "I wouldn't do that. There have been lot of grizzly bears spotted in the valley, and a woman was mauled last week by a mother grizzly." I responded the typical way most men would who don't think things through before opening their mouths, "Not a problem. It will be all right." The receptionist smiled, looked down at his desk, and shook his head. I headed out the door and into a brilliant, cloudless day.

The trail was right in front of me. I started my watch and off I went. Fantastic! Birds were singing! The air had a bit of a chill in it and smelled amazing! A runner's dream scenario!

That is, until about ten minutes into the run when I finally started to think about what the hotel clerk had said. My mind started playing out movie-type scenarios, and each scenario had me coming face-to-face with a 400 pound bundle of fur with sharp claws and bad breath. My mind started to embellish every noise and smell. The sound of birds alighting from a branch had me exaggerating their harmless noises into a potential full-out grizzly attack.

I started to think about escape strategies.

First strategy was to run serpentine because an equally stupid male once told me that bears could only run straight and could not change direction easily. However, I soon reasoned that if I were running side-to-side and the bear was running straight, wouldn't he catch me faster? And, if that happened, he would not be tired and would be able to eat me faster (true, I thought that!). Okay, that wouldn't work. I kept running—walking would make me an easier target.

Next, I thought if under attack, I would run straight into the river. (I used to swim competitively and would easily be able to out-swim the bear, which had now grown to over 800 kilos.) I looked over at the glacier-fed river rapids that were unmercifully pounding the rocks. Good plan, I thought, and I kept running.

Later, when I was recounting this story back at the hotel, between uncontrolled laughter from my colleagues, one of the rocket scientists in the group said, "Why didn't you just turn around and come back to the hotel when you were only ten minutes away?" (Good point, Einstein!)

About twenty minutes into the run, my salvation happened along! Up ahead, another trail crossed the one I was on. I was about twenty feet away from it when a very old man ran across the intersection. At the time, I was forty years old and in great shape. This guy was small, skinny, and...he was old! To top it off, he was wearing knee high black socks, a pair of old Adidas cotton shorts, and a ratty looking, white tee shirt.

In the split second that I saw him crossing the trail intersection, I had made this entire assessment of him, and the analytical realization that in the law of jungle survival, you only need to be faster than the slowest person in the group. So without any idea where the trail went that my salvation was running on, I got to the intersection a couple of seconds later and turned in behind him.

Now, with the bear bait only twenty short feet in front of me, I picked up the pace to close the distance. About ten seconds later, I realized the old man was still twenty feet in front of me. I picked up the pace. No change. I kicked it into high gear. No change in my situation. Every time I increased my pace, so did he! My attempt to catch my prey was now into its fifth minute, and we were flying along this magnificent mountain trail doing about a six-minute mile pace (fast enough to turn in a sub-forty minute 10K race time). My heart was pounding like a piston in a noisy locomotive; my lungs were burning, and my head was about to explode.

"This can't be happening!" I thought. "This guy is old!" I started reminding myself that I could run a marathon in three hours and nine minutes. My best time for a 10K is thirty-seven minutes.

Up ahead, the trail split into two directions. The old guy in front of me (apparently on steroids!) went right. I went left. My thought process was, "The pain of a grizzly attack has got to be better than the pain in every part of my body that I am experiencing at this moment!"

I significantly slowed down the pace and tried to recover as I attempted to figure out where I was and how to get back to the hotel.

About five minutes later, my body had somewhat recovered and I was confident that I was heading in the right direction (I figured no one ever needed to know about the old guy kicking my butt). And then, with the stealth of a jungle cat, the old guy was back! He effortlessly glided up beside me, smiled pleasantly, and in a very polite British accent, asked, "You staying at the hotel?" I replied, "Yes," so he asked, "Can I run back with you? I am a little bit lost." Outwardly, I smiled and said, "Sure thing." Inwardly, I said "Oh crap!"

After a few minutes, he started ever so slightly to edge ahead of me. I couldn't have that so I matched his pace. He picked it up. I matched. He picked it up again. I matched again. Arggh! We were doing it again! Racing along with that burning feeling creeping back into my lungs.

I stuttered out in between gasps for rarified air, "You're pretty fast." He replied, "I used to think so, but I had a dreadful race last week." Curious now, I asked, "What race were you in?" In a self-depreciative tone, he said, "I ran the London Marathon, and I was pathetic, so I am here to get some high altitude training." Now, I have to know, so I ask, "What was your time?" Annoyed with himself again, he says, "2:40." I almost choke! I blurt out, "Holy crap! How old are you?" He informs me that he is sixty-one and that he is ranked third in the world for long distance runners over age sixty.

If at that moment, a grizzly bear had happened along, he would have seen me looking pretty sheepish. About fifteen minutes previously, I had seen this nice old guy, who turned out to be a world-class athlete, flash in front of me, and in that instant—in that instant, I had made a total assessment about him and his capabilities. Was I wrong!

We ALL do it. And we do it within about three seconds. Our built-in people analysis machine sees a person we have never met before, and based on his or her height, weight, age, skin color, dress, etc., we make an instant assessment about the person's intelligence, abilities, background, wealth, etc.

As a leader, I learned that day that judgments about people without truly knowing about their capabilities, their passions, their motivations, and their pain are incredibly dangerous. I vowed to develop the discipline to seek always to understand every potential stakeholder I came across as a leader. I would fight every instinct within me to make snap judgments about people.

This vow paid off big-time for me eight years later while travelling in Eastern Europe. I was at the airport in Bucharest, Romania, heading to London, and riding a shuttle bus from the terminal building out to the airplane. Sitting beside me was a guy struggling with his Nokia Communicator (an old technology mobile handset—the precursor to the BlackBerry). The way he was dressed and his mannerisms would have most people immediately assessing him as an average Joe, who was frustrated with simple technology; probably, most people would have totally ignored him.

I had heard his British accent (Yes, another Brit—Here we go again!) so I knew I could "take the piss out of him" (British slang for having some fun with someone). I turned to him and said, "We have to get you a BlackBerry!" He laughed and replied, "Yah, that is what my team keeps saying, but I just can't let go of this thing."

We started talking. It turned out he was the Group CEO for a large multinational organization. We sat together on the plane for the three-hour flight to London, and by the time we landed, I had learned that his company was having an enormous sales problem that could drive the business into bankruptcy if it didn't get fixed. By the time I left him in London, we had a handshake agreement on a $600,000 contract to take over the leadership and management of doing a turn-around in his sales organization.

It would have been so easy to ignore him and go about my business like the majority of people on public transportation do. It would have been easy to let my instinctual situational analysis mechanism tell me that he was a "Nobody" and not to pay attention to him. However, I learned back in Canmore on that mountain trail running with that old grizzly bear that making snap judgments about people is dangerous.

Opportunities are everywhere. As a leader, learn to open your mind to learning as much as you can about employees, partners, vendors, customers, and prospects before you write them off.

You, your career, and your business will be far more successful for it.

What snap judgments in business have you made about people that have turned out to be dangerous or just plain wrong?

How can you avoid a "grizzly bear" attack from a snap judgment in the future?

What habits do you need to form about avoiding snap judgments?

CHAPTER 13

Being Downgraded and Other Micro Insults

"The single most important thing to remember about any enterprise is that there are no results inside its walls. The result of a business is a satisfied customer." — Peter Drucker

What is it like to be a customer in your business? Have you ever sat down and thought about that question? What is it like to experience every aspect of what your organization does? I know you probably do customer satisfaction surveys and maybe even transactional surveys. But why? What lasting, consistent changes do they help to create in the business? What freedom do they unleash for the team? How do you become a better customer serving organization because of the feedback?

When you bring on new employees, how much time do you spend with your new recruits, insuring they completely understand the principles for serving a client with purpose?

Disney spends six weeks doing it. Lulu Lemon does the same.

I am hyper-passionate about customer service. I have been called an "evangelist" about it.

Customers, after all, pay our salaries. That's true for all of us.

As a leader, you have to ooze passion for the customer so exuberance for the customer is shared by the entire team.

As a CEO or any other executive, I have always said, "I am the head customer service agent!"

To that end, when I see or experience customer service that is not up to my expectations, I am all over it. I rationalize that the best gift an organization can receive is a complaint. It is a gift because the business gets to do something about it and make sure it never happens again. Not all businesses, though, view complaints as gifts. Let me tell you another personal story to illustrate how a customer feels when a business and its employees don't provide proper customer service.

In August 2004, my family and I were moving to Europe. My wife was nervously excited. My ten-year-old son, Grant, was very excited. And my fourteen-year old daughter, Denielle, informed me that I was destroying her life. As for me, I was just nervous.

Packing up and moving halfway across the world to the unknown by yourself is one thing, but with your family for an unknown period of time, to an unknown new life is....There are no words for it.

I remember us sitting at the Vancouver airport. My wife and son are excited. My daughter is doing her best to give me her "I hate you; you have ruined my life" stare. (Teenagers—I recommend them to every business leader on the planet. There is nothing better to help you develop super high emotional intelligence! More about the value of teenagers later in the book.)

We board the Lufthansa flight from Vancouver to Frankfurt. The company with which I have accepted a new turn-around assignment is good to us. We all get to fly business class. Once onboard, we are all excited, except for my daughter, who continues her look of disgust (except when she thinks I'm not looking; then she settles into the princess role of a business class world jet-setter).

Just after we are airborne, we discover that the in-seat entertainment system is down and my son's seat is broken so it cannot be made into a flat bed as advertised. No big deal, but since he wants the full experience, I change places with him. No big deal all around except that the flight attendants take on this air of "It's not our fault" (even though no one was blaming them for anything).

The rest of the flight progresses with kids complaining about no TV to watch and smaller micro-insults from the staff—I call them micro-insults because they are the kind of customer service experiences that get under your skin. We've all had them. They are what happen when service organizations do not spend the time to train and inspect their teams and thoroughly craft their processes to ensure they deliver a consistent level of service equal or surpassing what we were promised when we signed on as their customers.

We have to overnight in Frankfurt. The family is exhausted, so we spend a quiet evening at the airport hotel having dinner and catching up on sleep.

The next morning, we excitedly head back to the airport to check in for the last leg of our journey.

What happens next is, even to this day, hard to comprehend in the world of service.

We walk up to the business class check-in counter. I present our passports. The agent behind the counter says with a German accent, "Good morning, Mr. Murray. We have been expecting you." I immediately think, "Wow! This is impressive!" She continues, "You have been downgraded." Not sure I heard correctly what I thought I had just heard, I reply, "Pardon me?" She responds again, "You have been downgraded. Our flight is full and we don't have room for you and your family in business class. We have seats for you in economy." Stay calm, Bob. Stay calm. I mention that we have full fare business class tickets and ask, "How are you going to compensate my company for the difference they paid?" She replies, "It's not my fault. There is nothing I can do." I then tell her that since we have full fare business class tickets, I would like to cancel my tickets, get a full refund, and then buy economy class tickets. She tells me, "That's impossible; the flight is full."

Argh! Okay, being reasonable, I ask her what she can do. She tells me that all she can do is issue me the boarding passes, and then I can take up the issue with the supervisor at the gate. Done.

Boarding passes in hand, we head to the departure gates. Up ahead is airport security. There is a massive line-up for the economy class security check while no one is in the business or fast track security line-up. So, since we have full fare business class tickets, we head for that line. The guard at that security check asks for our boarding passes. After he examines them, and sounding like Arnold Schwarzenegger in *The Terminator*, he says, "This is the business class line. You are economy. Go over there." As he points to the back of the massive queue in the other line, I say, "You don't understand. I have a business class ticket." As he responds, he literally pulls a machine gun from around his back to the front, "You don't understand. Other line, over there!"

I get the point. We head over to the other line. Time ticks by and my blood pressure is rising. We get through security and arrive at our gate. Frustrated, my wife, Colleen, gathers the kids into chairs far away from the gate desk.

At the gate desk, I ask to see the supervisor. A guy, who introduces himself as the manager, comes along. I go through the whole song and dance again, even though he has obviously been briefed about my issue. I keep my cool because I know there is no point in losing it. He, on cue, tells me there is nothing he can do. It is not his fault. I explain over again that I have rights to compensation and I could cancel my ticket, get a refund, and buy an economy class ticket. Without any sign of sympathy, he tells me that the flight is full. By now, the gate agents are calling final boarding for the flight. The unyielding Lufthansa manager in front of me then says, in his broken German-English accent, "Do you want to go to your destination or not?" Exasperated and in need to get to Bucharest to start work the next day, I wave over to Colleen and we board the bus for the ride out to the airplane.

The bus pulls up to the plane's stairs. We are the last passengers to board. As I enter the door, I look into the business class cabin and notice about eight empty seats. I don't say anything, but I am sure the look on my face is that of total disgust. We keep walking toward our assigned seats in the economy class cabin. I sit down and begin to settle in.

I feel a tap on my shoulder. I look up to see a man standing in front of me wearing an airline captain's uniform. I immediately start to think, "Bravo! Someone has come to his senses and is going to apologize to me for one of the worst airline experiences I have ever had."

The captain leans down to my face level, just centimeters from my nose, and says in his very self-important tone, "Mr. Murray, we are *not* going to have any *problems* with you, are we?" Unbelievable. I am speechless (which doesn't happen very often). I stammer out, "Pardon me?" He repeats his question, this time with more inflection and more annoyance. "No," I reply. "There's nothing further for me to say."

The plane takes off and we land in our new home without any further events worth mentioning.

As I continue to feel frustrated, however, I realize the manager at the gate obviously radioed the captain and briefed him that I was not happy. The company's communication processes are obviously working. But they are working to make life easier for the company—not the customer.

A couple of days after the flight, I am still fuming and intent on getting the company to issue a refund for the price of the business class tickets. After work one day, I go to the local Lufthansa office. I arrive at five minutes to five in the afternoon. "No problem," I think. "The office will be open until five." I grab the door handle and pull. Locked. I see staff inside so I knock on the door. A man inside, wearing a Lufthansa uniform, looks up and waves at me to go away. I knock again. This time louder. This time, with the look of total annoyance, the man gets up and walks abruptly to the door, unlocks it, opens it just enough to stick his head out the door, and begins to yell at me in Romanian. I interrupt him, by saying, "English, please." This gets better and better. He then starts to yell at me in English, but this time, he also takes his hand and slides it across his throat—the international hand sign for, "You're dead."

I am sure he was just having a bad day.

I stay cool and politely ask him for a phone number so I can call his superiors. He looks stunned and asks, "What can I help you with?" I quickly explain the situation and ask him what I can do next. I am still standing outside. He has still got his face stuck out the slim opening in the door. He says, "Wait here." He closes the door, locks it, and walks away. A few moments later, he comes back with an email address for the airline's claims department, hands the paper to me, closes the door, locks it, and walks away.

I file a claim later that evening.

After three months and multiple follow-up emails, I receive a cheque in the mail for the refund of the business class ticket, minus the economy ticket value. No apology. No request to come fly Lufthansa's friendly skies again.

Since that flight in the summer of 2004, I have, as of the date I am writing, taken over hundred more transcontinental flights. All the flights in business class. Each flight on average costs $2,500. My whole family has been with me on sixteen of those flights. My wife alone has been with me for twenty others. Colleen has herself taken sixteen flights on her own. Add them all up and you have 184 flights. Total value: over $460,000. Not one of those flights has been with Lufthansa.

Disrespecting your customers has a tangible cost. The intangible cost of brand image and negative messages are beyond calculation. Plus, I have told this story as a keynote speaker probably to well over 25,000 people.

How could Lufthansa have handled the situation differently?

First, realize that customers really don't care whose fault it is. At the end of the day, they just want someone to own the problem. They do not want to hear anyone in the organization say, "It's not my fault" or listen to someone attempt to blame someone else. They want to see you doing everything you can—with authenticity.

MBA schools don't spend enough time, if any, on the whole concept of serving your customer.

As a leader, wrap your head around the customer being everything. Ensure that your team values customers just as much. When you or your team delivers less than your company promises, recover swiftly, and surely. When a customer complains, it truly is a gift so receive it like the best gift you ever got and blow the client away with your sincere recovery. Make changes in process and training so it does not happen again.

If an amazing, replicable customer experience is to be, it is up to you.

Again I ask you, what is it like to be a customer in your business?

Sit down and think about that question. What is it like to experience every aspect of what your organization does?

What is every single customer experience like at every touch point?

How could that experience be designed and delivered to be replicable?

CHAPTER 14

Under-React in Crisis

"The Chinese use two brush strokes to write the word 'crisis.' One brush stroke stands for danger; the other for opportunity. In a crisis, be aware of the danger—but recognize the opportunity."
— John F. Kennedy

Kennedy's little bit of leadership advice is not hard-wired in most people, let alone most leaders. The natural hard wiring and software we all have on board is built around the fight-or-flight response developed through a couple of hundred thousand years of evolution. Neither do program downloads into our brain's operating system over time—from parents, friends, classrooms, and "the street"—usually prepare us for this level of emotional intelligence.

For most of us, a crisis still activates the primitive fight-or-flight response that has us naturally jumping into action to protect ourselves, those around us, or our assets. Most inexperienced leaders thrive on the "command and control" opportunity that a crisis presents. They will jump up, become highly directive, and spout orders like some kind of mad dictator.

That is, unless they understand that true leaders under-react in a crisis.

On July 19th, 1989, United Airlines flight 232 had lifted off from Denver en route to Philadelphia via Chicago. The flight crew leveled off the massive 165 ton DC 10 aircraft at 29,000 feet, autopilot was set, and they were about to savor their coffee and enjoy the gorgeous, cloudless summer day over the Midwest United States.

Without notice, an enormous explosive sound came from behind them, and the aircraft experienced a violent shuddering. Later, they would learn that the explosion they heard was their tail engine (engine # 2) suffering a catastrophic turbine fan failure that separated into seventy pieces of high-speed shrapnel and perforated the tail and elevator section of the aircraft. The explosion was so loud that it was heard on the ground some five miles below.

Captain Al Haynes immediately asked his co-pilot to take control of the airplane so he could assess the situation. The #1 rule for pilots during an "event" is: Fly the airplane, get it under control, and find the nearest airport. It became instantly apparent that the plane had lost the number two engine. Instinctively, the flight crew's training kicked in and they initiated the sequence to shut down the damaged engine. A DC 10 has three engines, so the pilots were not worried that the plane could stay aloft with the remaining power it had. The first sign of more serious problems, however, was the second engine's throttle and fuel lever were frozen in position and could not be moved.

The co-pilot then reported an even more distressing problem. He could not keep the aircraft straight and level. He attempted different throttle settings on the remaining engines, but that made the situation worse. The second co-pilot then reported that they had lost the hydraulic fluid not only in their primary system, but in the two redundant systems as well.

In large commercial aircrafts, the pilot's controls are tied into either electric motors that control the moveable flight surfaces or hydraulic systems that achieve the same effect. United Airlines Flight 232's explosive engine failure, and the subsequent shrapnel shower, had perforated the tail section of the airplane and cut through all three hydraulic systems—an event that computer models would later calculate had a one in one billion chance of happening. The pilots of the big jet had no ability to control ailerons, which effect rolling, the elevators that control pitching up and down, the rudder that controls yaw or side-to-side movement, the spoilers that slow the plane down, or the flaps and slats that make the much needed change to the shape of the wing for landing. In short, here they were with 295 people on board and hurtling through the air at 500 miles per hour, and out of control! With 30,000 pounds of jet fuel on board, they were now, in effect, a missile. If they were able to land, they had no steering and no brakes.

The crippled jet was wildly porpoising up and down—going from sharp dives to steep climbs, and dangerously trying to roll over on its back. The pilots quickly discovered that by using the throttles on the two remaining engines, they were able to keep the plane from rolling over and to somewhat control the porpoising, but the aircraft was still flying in large right-hand turns and losing altitude like a giant cork screw.

Three minutes into the crisis, Captain Haynes got on the radio and declared an emergency. As a pilot myself, I know you do not declare an emergency without exhausting all possibilities that you can land safely on your own. Declaring an emergency is not taken lightly by pilots.

The response: Flight 232 was handed a separate radio channel and given to a dedicated controller to stay with its crew. Flight controllers never question a pilot in an emergency. Their experience and training kicks in. They have an amazing ability to talk clearly, calmly, and competently—making pilots in trouble feel like there is hope. When a pilot is in trouble, the first thing the pilot and the controller want to do is to get the plane on the ground by finding a suitable airport. With the data of Flight 232's crazy trajectory now showing up on radar, they quickly figured that the giant circle they were flying in and the altitude they were losing would get them close to a small airport in Sioux City, Iowa.

This is the cool leadership lesson….

Within minutes of the emergency being declared and the location of the "crash" (That's what everyone on the ground thought after hearing what the problem was) identified, a carefully architected response plan was enacted. Two local hospitals in Sioux City were alerted and a call went out for every available nurse and doctor. State Troopers closed the freeway in case United 232 had to attempt to land there. Over 200 National Guard troops were called out to the airport. Local fire departments all rolled to various locations in the area, ready in case the plane crashed somewhere else. United Airlines filled an empty jet with all available personnel in Chicago and were in the air to Sioux City even while Flight 232 was still making its way there. Maintenance personnel from United and competitor American Airlines in San Francisco and Chicago stopped everything and were on the phone with each other, pouring over schematic drawings in an attempt to find a solution.

Back in the air, Captain Haynes and his crew were now joined by another United Airlines captain who happened to be a passenger on board the crippled plane. When Captain Dennis Fitch entered the cockpit, he was quickly in complete disbelief. Captain Haynes gave him the job of taking over the throttles that were the only method of controlling the plane so he could watch the main flight indicator gauges. The other two pilots on the flight deck were handling ground communications and researching solutions in flight manuals.

Here is the leadership in crisis lesson that takes years to master: Remain calm and collected. Your team members need to see you under control. They need to know you are working toward a solution. They want to know what you want them to do. You have to be rock solid.

If you listen to cockpit voice recordings from United Airlines Flight 232's last thirty minutes, Captain Haynes never loses his temper. His voice always stays calm and collected. He has resolve. At times, he keeps his sense of humour by suggesting to the flight crew that "Although I do not drink, I may start today." He mentions to the ground controller many times to give him directions to keep the plane away from populated areas.

About twenty minutes before their planned "landing" in Sioux City, Captain Haynes called the head flight attendant, Jan Brown Lohr, to the flight deck. When she arrived, the captain very briefly, but competently, informed Jan of the situation and exactly what he wanted her to do. Ms. Brown Lohr afterward said that when she left and closed the cockpit door, she had absolute confidence that they were going to make it to Sioux City and they would survive. Asked why she felt that way, she replied that she sensed the captain had it under control and was executing a plan.

Jan Brown Lohr then went into the passenger cabin and instructed each flight attendant individually and quietly so as to not panic the passengers. They had thirty unescorted children onboard that day so she then went around the cabin and moved adults who were flying by themselves to sit with each child and gave the new guardian instructions to stay with the child and help him or her exit the plane. Finally, she went to every exit row and moved passengers whom she felt would not be able to open exit doors—replacing them with those she thought were able-bodied individuals who looked like they had leadership abilities.

The most important thing leaders do in a crisis after communicating is to let people on the team do their jobs. Trusting that they understand their roles and the gravity of the situation, they do not micromanage them to the point of rebellion and second-guessing.

Forty-four minutes after the second engine ruptured, flight 232 was lined up for final approach into the Sioux City airport. A normal approach speed for a fully loaded DC 10 is 161 miles an hour. Flight 232 was not able to slow down its speed and was coming in at 247 miles an hour. In a normal landing approach, a DC 10 descends at a rate of about 300 feet per minute. Flight 232 was losing 1,800 feet per minute. Just as it was about to touch down, the right wing dipped and hit the ground, causing the jet to cartwheel violently down the runway. The fuselage broke into five pieces and came to rest in a cornfield.

Of the 295 people on board, 111 perished from either the trauma or smoke inhalation. Miraculously, 184 people survived—thirteen people walked away from the accident without a scratch.

The outcome would not have been as good (if you can say that), if it had not been for the leadership of Captain Haynes. Rock solid resolve. Thorough communication. A plan people understood. Responsibilities clearly defined. And...he let his team do their jobs without panic—without micro-management.

Under-react in a crisis.

What kind of crisis scenario is most likely for your business?

What can you do to be prepared so you can under-react and lead your team?

CHAPTER 15

Overreact to Values Violations

"If we are to go forward, we must go back and rediscover those precious values—that all reality hinges on moral foundations and that all reality has spiritual control." — Dr. Martin Luther King, Jr.

An organization's values are its core fabric, the soul that holds a business together and guides it through good times and periods of difficulties. When leadership ignores guiding values through its own ignorance or lack of integrity, anarchy is just around the corner. When the team behaves in ways that are against the company's values, the business is doomed for a culture of entitlement, disloyal customers, and weak performance or failure.

A lot of inexperienced leaders will not make a "big deal" when they witness the very core values of the organization being ignored, violated, or disrespected. They will allow little "indiscretions" to go unchecked—thinking, "It's not that bad. Don't make a big deal."

They do not teach this dismissal of values violations in business school. Vital leadership strength has to come from having rock solid values yourself that align with the business you are in, understanding the power within your team and the team at large within the business. Such leadership strength is counterintuitive in a lot of cultures. But it is a key part of the emotional intelligence that has to be developed through mentoring, experience, and trial by fire.

A leader whom people will follow on almost any journey is one who protects the values of an organization as if they were a priceless, vanishing commodity. The leader protects those values by "walking the values talk," and through never, ever tolerating any violation of the values.

In 2004, I moved my family to Romania to take on a very cool turn-around sales leadership assignment with a new wireless mobile entrant. The business would later be purchased by Vodafone, one of the largest and most successful mobile communications companies in the world. Part of the reason for purchasing the business and paying five times the share value was that the business was a shining example of a well-run organization with a very engaged culture and extremely satisfied customers.

Romania was then a country that struggled with corruption at every level of government and in some of its businesses. The accepted norm among the people was "This is the way it has always been, and it is not going to change, so you might as well get what you can, while you can." Bribes and grey and black market activity were a normal way of doing business.

I was responsible for turning around the company's sales organization. The "turn-around" was not because of poor performance. On the contrary. The business had been wildly successful because of incredible market demand. Now, however, the market was becoming saturated, so the sales team needed to know how to sell in tough times and in a replicable way. I had a team of 400 highly educated and very energetic twenty-somethings. They were revered by their friends and family for landing such amazing jobs. Most of them were making more money than both of their parents combined. They were like sponges when it came to learning about business, and they eagerly did everything to please their customers and win business. They really were a dream team.

Shortly after arriving and settling into my new role, I was sitting at my desk one day when I noticed through my office door that no one was at his or her desk on the sales floor. "Strange," I thought since it was late afternoon so the office was normally busy with account managers writing up their orders for the day. Curiosity got the best of me so I got up to see where everyone was.

When I stuck my head out the door, I noticed a massive group of sales reps and support staff grouped around one particular desk near the door. There was a carnival atmosphere similar to what you would see during a great sale in a discount store. People were pushing and grabbing at something, but I couldn't quite make out what was happening. As I walked over and asked what was going on, one of the guys turned and told me, with a big smile on his face, that someone had brought in a box of pirated videos and was selling them for $1 each. I waded into the centre of the action and discovered about 200 pirated DVD's in a big pile on the table. I quickly threw up my hands in the air and yelled, "Everyone, stop!" Instant silence. (I may be small, but when I raise my voice, people notice right away!) With visible agitation on my face, I ordered everyone to put back the DVD's they had bought, for money to be refunded, and for the pirated merchandise to be removed from the property within sixty seconds or immediate terminations would start. I looked at my three sales directors, who were in the middle of the action, and I sternly told them to get into my office! I turned and walked away.

Back in my office, after all three sales directors had joined me, I closed the door and went "Bobzilla." (*Bobzilla rarely comes out, but once released from his cage, no one messes with him. Bobzilla always appears when the company's values have been violated.*)

I reiterated to the directors that I never again wanted to see pirated merchandise on company premises. I was on a roll because I talked about how we would never be involved in any activity that was illegal or immoral—including the paying of bribes for contracts. Halfway through my tantrum, one of the directors was brave enough (or stupid enough) to say, "What's the big deal? Everyone does it." I then asked my sales directors, "Would you be okay with someone stealing a few hundred of our handsets and activation codes to get free mobile service?" They said, "No. That would be stealing." Incredulously, the lights still didn't go on in their heads. They started to tell me that I was being unreasonable and that the team needed "to cut loose" every once in awhile.

Slow learners!

They then threw out to me that business may be done that way in North America, but this was Eastern Europe. I reminded them that their job as leaders was to protect the brand and values of the organization, and that we were going to be recognized as the leaders in a business that everyone from vendors to partners and customers could trust.

Still more debate. "Unbelievable!" I thought.

"Okay, how about this," I said. "If you cannot get your heads wrapped around leading our values and protecting our brand, go pack up your desks and find another place to work."

Amazing! The message was finally received.

Values are priceless. Your job as a leader is to make sure they are never violated or even bent in little ways. And if you have to overreact in order to protect them, that is part of your job as well.

What are your company's values?

Are they something that remains on the boardroom wall, or are they revered in the organization as sacred?

What values violations—big or small—are happening in your business? How are you going to be a leader by turning around that situation?

CHAPTER 16

Being Arrested in Hong Kong - Values Based Practical Leadership

"It's only a cut, a reminder of this day. A reminder to ask every day, Why am I doing this?" — Victor Robert Lee

Values are the critical set of guiding principles nurtured within us by parents, family, relatives, chosen friends, teachers, coaches, and people we admire—they are our "golden rules." Your grandmother probably said to you, "If you don't have anything nice to say, you shouldn't say anything at all." That was her way of teaching you the value of respect (for others and yourself).

Values are also those things that you, quite frankly, value in your life. Like your family, loved ones, reputation, being viewed as someone who is honest, helpful, trustworthy, hardworking, etc. The television news and daily newspapers are packed with politicians, sports stars, and celebrities who have crossed a line and had their names and reputations ruined because they either lacked or violated their values.

As an example, one of my top values is freedom. I never realized how much it meant to me and how important it was for me truly to live in harmony with my values until it was once briefly taken away.

I used to wonder why in some work situations I could not get over the feeling of being trapped. That feeling always hit me when I was confronted with a manager who was hugely dictatorial or unfocused. What usually happened was the manager would be heavily micro-managing me on the most ridiculous details. I would get frustrated but never really understood why. As a result, I would often morph into all kinds of unrecognizable people in order somehow to appease the autocrat who was out-of-control.

Then it hit me in a very memorable way—and this is a very hard story for me to tell because of the feelings that it brings back.

I was on a flight from Vancouver to Mumbai for a client project. I was flying with the remarkable airline Cathay Pacific and had to change planes in Hong Kong. There was absolutely nothing unusual about the flight from Vancouver to Hong Kong, other than the outstanding service from the Cathay Pacific team. When I arrived in Hong Kong, I had to, like all passengers, go through another security screening. It was 7 p.m. and I had a scant thirty minutes to catch my connecting flight to Mumbai. At the security-screening checkpoint, I routinely removed my laptop and liquids from my carry-on bag and placed my belongings onto the conveyor belt leading to the x-ray machine. When I stepped through the metal detector, an awaiting security guard asked me "Is this carry-on bag yours" as she pointed to my carry-on bag that had now been pulled aside. I replied that it was. She asked me whether I was carrying scissors. I replied that I was not. She asked whether she could look inside. Naturally, I agreed. She looked around inside my bag, removed a few items, and then took the bag back for another x-ray.

My carry-on bag rolled through the x-ray machine, and once again, as she was looking at the computer screen, she asked me whether I had scissors in the bag. I again replied that I did not. She pivoted the computer screen around so I could see it and pointed at a pair of long, pointy end scissors clearly showing on the screen. I said, "That looks like scissors." The security guard then unceremoniously removed every one of my worldly possessions from my bag, then grabbed the inside liner, and callously ripped the liner from the carry-on bag.

There, inside the liner of my bag, was a magazine that, upon further examination, contained a pair of scissors that had been meticulously taped inside the magazine.

After the original horror of seeing what had been somehow, yet methodically, placed inside the liner of my carry-on bag, I instinctively switched to denial; after all, the scissors were not mine and I had no idea how they got into my bag. A denial that I am sure, you, if you had been the security guard, would have had a hard time believing.

The next thing I knew, a parade of various uniformed and non-uniformed police and security personnel converged upon the screening area. I was pulled aside as a volley of seemingly never-ending questions began. In my ignorance, I honestly thought; "This is a misunderstanding. The scissors are not mine. I have no idea how they got there. Let's just let me pack up my belongings, which are scattered all over a table, and I'll be on my way to my next flight."

The next eight hours proved my naïve thinking so completely wrong!

Next came handcuffs and being led by a posse of policemen through the terminal to a small room somewhere in the airport's bowels. There began eight hours of interrogation. I was asked every possible question that one could possibly imagine right down to what my sexual orientation was. They wanted to know what each and every vitamin supplement, Advil, shaving cream bottle, and everything else in my bag was for. They asked for my computer password and then went through each and every file on my laptop, pausing occasionally to ask me who was in pictures, who was who, etc.

Just like in a Hollywood movie, a good cop and a bad cop took turns talking to me. The good cop was a decent guy who kept telling me not to panic (I must have looked as rattled as I felt), but then the bad cop would step in and tell me I was going to a Chinese prison for a very long time.

At various points in the evening, I would ask whether I could call my embassy. My friend, the bad cop, would laugh and say in broken English, "Where do you think you are? You have no rights here!" I asked repeatedly whether I could use the toilet until I finally told the good cop, "If you don't take me to a toilet very soon, I won't be able to hold it any longer." He discussed the potential security risk with the other policemen for a couple of minutes and then came over and told me he would take me to the toilet. So off we went, with three new "friends" watching over me, to the bathroom where they took an extreme interest in me relieving myself. Then it was back to the little room for more questions.

Close to midnight, another band of merry police officers took me down to the arrivals area (still in handcuffs) to go through my checked luggage, pulled from my connecting flight, which had left hours earlier. After I was asked to open the bag, they all stood back as if the bag were going to explode when I inserted the key into the lock. Once my suitcase was opened, they took turns taking each and every item out of my bag and laying it out on the floor. The contents of my bag (a week's worth of clothing, workout gear, and a bottle of wine as a gift for the client I was going to see) eventually covered a space on the floor in the middle of the Arrivals Hall about 10 by 10 feet. Once they were satisfied that nothing illegal was in my checked bag, they instructed me to repack my bag while I was still handcuffed.

Back to my little room for more thought-provoking questions and to be told by the bad cop that I was being charged with attempting to bring a concealed weapon onto an aircraft. I was horrified. The bad cop had a sly smile on his face—he was having a very good time on what otherwise would have been a very boring night for him. He said I would be brought to a holding cell and taken before a magistrate in the morning.

I sunk into the most depressed feeling I had ever experienced. I felt completely drained. I kept going through scenarios in my mind about how the magazine and scissors could have got in my bag. I had been on five international flights in the last two weeks to three other continents. My carry-on bag was out of my site a few times during that period. I kept racking my brain for something that would make sense. Nothing came to me.

Then at 3 a.m., the good cop came into the room, said something in Chinese to the bad cop, and came over to tell me they were not pressing charges and I was free to go. What? I sat there stunned. At first, I thought it was a joke. I asked him again. He replied that they believed I was telling the truth and someone had obviously placed the item in my bag as a joke or to get me into trouble.

They took the handcuffs off me and took me to immigration where I was processed as a visitor in Hong Kong and let go. Dumbfounded, I wandered out into the airport as a free man, attempting to get my thoughts together. I found a hotel nearby and gladly paid the $500 for a room, thinking I would feel better after a good night's sleep.

I called my wife, and for the first time in eight hours, completely let my emotions loose as the impact of what had just happened hit me hard. There was not a wink of sleep that night. When the sun came up, I got dressed, entered a gorgeous, cloudless morning, and went for a run. Even though I was in a foreign country, I never felt so free at any other time in my life than I did at that moment.

I discovered a tremendous amount about myself and my value set that morning while I was out running. I realized how important it is to understand one's most important values and to protect them in order to achieve happiness. I recognized how critical the value of freedom was to me and it dawned on me why, at some moments in my life, I felt so incredibly smothered when I was being micro-managed or constrained by ridiculous bureaucracy. I reminded myself over and over again how blessed I was to have the friends, family, and life I had. I was so fortunate to have my health. I was very proud that I have always lived my life with integrity and there is absolutely nothing about my past that would potentially embarrass me in front of anyone.

Leading by your values is critical to being a successful leader in today's world. Living your values is equally critical to your happiness and fulfillment. When you are asked to violate your personal values, you will discover that your health and happiness will suffer and any compensation paid to you will not make up for that.

Values are critical to organizations as well. It is so very important that leaders within the business live the company's values. It is equally important to you as a leader within your company to ensure that the organization's values and their people align with your values. If they do not, you will be constantly "pushing water uphill."

Be tireless about recruiting, assessing, hiring, onboarding, and developing only those employees who align with the company's values and culture. If you do not, you will discover a painful employee termination lies in the future.

Companies have seen revenue, profitability, and market share erased because some executive took the easy road, whether it be through bribes, faulty products, or questionable business practices. Or he completely demoralized the company's workforce—the most important asset in the company—because leaders' actions don't match company rhetoric.

Most organizations will have a "Values Statement" posted on the boardroom wall. With most organizations, that statement is probably the only place where the company values are seen, and, again, very few in the company talk about values regularly. Enron, the infamous electricity brokerage house of the 1990s, had a value statement on its boardroom wall. The first word on the list was "Integrity." The CEO, CFO, and others are now serving lengthy jail terms for a $42 billion fraud scheme.

Violating your values or those of the people you are entrusted to lead has only one outcome—and it is not good! Violating your company's values will destroy your brand and culture, and it will cost you in lost revenue, productivity, customer satisfaction, and increased costs. Your responsibility as a leader is always, without fail, to protect *ferociously* your personal values and those of the people and business you lead.

Violating your own personal values will cause damage to your brand, your reputation, your relationships, your family, and, eventually, your health.

My top five personal values are (in order):

Freedom

Integrity

Health and Wellness

Family (including Friends)

Being able to lead and teach

Some will ask me why my family is not the first priority. My reasoning is this: If I cannot live my life feeling that I am free to decide and do as I see fit, then I cannot fully love. If I cannot stay true to who I am and be a "man of my word," the people I care dearly about in my life will have little reason to respect who I am. And...if I do not have my health, then I will be in no condition to give everything of myself to my family. My family and friends actually get a *way* better version of me when I am in sync with my values.

I have also discovered that when I am living in total harmony with my highest values, my energy, passion, and enthusiasm for everything is virtually unlimited! There is no such thing as "Thank God, it's Friday" in my vocabulary. I do not dread Mondays. I can't wait to get each and every day started!

When any one of my top values is threatened or marginalized by something I have chosen to take on, I discover my energy and enthusiasm is also downgraded from an "eleven" out of ten. I am not myself and everyone around me feels it too.

What are your top values? Take some time and list them in order...

1.

2.

3.

4.

5.

Now, are you living your highest values or are you spending the majority of your time serving lesser values? When are you at your happiest? When is your energy, passion, and enthusiasm at its lowest levels?

Every person on the planet wants to—whether or not he or she consciously knows it—live in alignment with his or her highest values. I call this living your personal "why." If, as a leader, you understand that need and seek to connect with your team members in ways that show how following you also serves their personal why, you will have inspired them to move forward.

As leaders, we often have an advantage over our followers because we are given more data and information. We are given the luxury of time (so we have our "why" figured out). Unfortunately, the people who have to make change happen rarely get all the information or the luxury of time to figure out that the planned journey is going to be fulfilling for them.

Understanding that everyone has a "why" and communicating to your team members what is in it for them will bring amazing results.

CHAPTER 17

LBWA—The Things You Find Out from Truly Listening to the Frontline!

"When one has the feeling of dislike for evil, when one feels tranquil, one finds pleasure in listening to good teachings; when one has these feelings and appreciates them, one is free of fear."

— Buddha

Leadership by Walking Around—LBWA. Funny thing. LBWA is probably the most effective leadership tool on the planet, and yet, it is the least practiced.

The helpful stuff I have found out just from simply and religiously doing daily walks around the office or building and stopping by to talk to each and every single employee! I always try to acknowledge someone for an important event. CLUE: If someone has a flower arrangement on her desk, it just might be a special occasion! Ask an employee about a picture on his desk or on her screensaver.

If you know someone who has achieved a big target, congratulate him on it. Ask him how he did it? Who on the team helped? What roadblocks or issues did he encounter? How could things be done better? What things around the business "piss him off?"

Walking around provides a massive opportunity to catch team members doing things right! Another lost leadership trait—actually looking to learn from the frontline and recognize its members for a great customer service act, a time saving process, or a perfect execution on a task. Good leaders know the advantage of this simple tool. Managers, on the other hand, rarely walk around, and when they do, they are fixated upon "catching" people screwing up.

It's hard to believe, but I see so many leaders, managers actually, full of their own self-importance, walking by employees every day, and not even saying, "Good morning." I had a peer once in Europe who would go visit one of our satellite offices and wait in his car until the manager he intended to visit came out to the car. They would have their meeting in the car and then he would leave. What a wasted opportunity for richness!

I blow away my team of leaders who report to me all the time by asking them about issues on the frontline they don't even know about themselves.

I hear from leaders all the time that, "I have 150 people in my business, and it is impossible to speak with all of them!" More crap! I have had 1,500 employees before, but I knew something about each and every one of them. I worked with a CEO once who had 25,000 employees, and it amazed me that he seemed to know the names of each and every one of them. He specialized in coming into the office on Christmas morning and handing out presents to team members who had mission critical jobs and needed to be there 24/7.

All it takes is an understanding that each and every team member has a brain, which when engaged, can come up with ingenious solutions to problems that big consulting firms charge thousands of dollars a day to unravel.

Next, it takes discipline—both from a planning perspective and from an execution aspect. Once you start doing it every day, it becomes part of your daily habit—like brushing your teeth. Make it your afternoon stretch or the first thing you do each morning. Stop, acknowledge, ask how the person is doing, and simply listen. Don't tell. Just listen. Ask another question and listen. Wish the person a fantastic day and move on. Capture the good stuff on suggestions and opportunities, and make sure you investigate and report on your findings and decisions.

This simple act will bring dividends back in terms of employee engagement that all the HR programs on the planet cannot match. It will bring you real solutions. It will make your employees see you as approachable and make them know that you care. Soon, employees will be coming to your door to ask how you are and whether there is anything you need (Not that that is why you do LBWA).

Go for a walk around your business today. Then write down five things you learned about your employees you didn't know before that can help your business to grow:

1. _____

2. _____

3. _____

4. _____

5. _____

CHAPTER 18

Never Walk Past Corporate Graffiti

"As the soil, however rich it may be, cannot be productive without cultivation, so the mind without culture can never produce good fruit." — Seneca

At Disneyland theme parks, a piece of litter does not stay on the ground anywhere in the park for more than seven seconds.

Malcolm Gladwell in his book, *The Tipping Point*, has pointed out that if graffiti is sprayed onto a building or city wall and it is allowed to stay there for a period of one week, more graffiti will soon follow. Similarly, if a window is broken on an abandoned (or occupied) building, and it is not repaired within one week, more broken windows will appear.

Graffiti may be viewed by some as "art," but for the majority, it is a sign of decay and social breakdown. So too in business. A business' culture is the organization's very soul. And any breakdown, or decay allowed to happen in the culture that does not align with the company's values, leads to further decay and social breakdown.

It is a leader's job to protect and foster the culture with all his or her might. In the case of an organization that has a morally bankrupt culture, it is the leader's job to rescue the culture and get it healthy again. Without a functional culture that aligns with the values of the people and the company, there can be no engagement among the team, no lasting loyalty to the customers, and likewise, no loyalty from the customers.

When New York Mayor Rudolph Giuliani wanted to clean up crime in the city, he started in the simplest of places—the subway system. New York's subway system is a massive web of underground tunnels and tracks that connect the population with the city and their homes. Before the initiative, the subway trains were a mess of multi-colored graffiti and filthy car interiors. An enormous related problem was people riding the system without paying the fare or being "gate jumpers"—those who would simply jump over the turnstiles rather than pay for the service.

Mayor Giuliani set up two graffiti squads to tackle the problem. One solution was to remove all graffiti on the trains. As a train made its way through the system and arrived at its turn-around point, a team would be waiting to remove quickly any graffiti that was applied to the train during its journey. Graffiti was never allowed to remain on a train. Within weeks, trains were making it all the way through the system without any new graffiti being applied. The trains were kept spotlessly clean inside and out.

Second, a large "graffiti" team of police officers was set up at stations to catch those avoiding not paying the fare. They even converted old buses into mobile processing centres because in the beginning, the numbers caught not paying were huge. There was zero tolerance.

The fare jumper project results were similar to the outcomes of the graffiti removal project—fare jumpers all but disappeared. The bigger news was that overall petty crime on the subway system drastically declined. Oddly, so too did major crime within the city.

In 2002, I took over leadership of a major call centre business. We had operations in over twenty Canadian communities and over 1,500 employees. The business was in desperate shape with high costs, low employee engagement, and low customer satisfaction. Not a recipe for long-term sustainability. After a short period of discovery, I found some smaller centres in remote communities were outstanding performers. The problem was the larger centres in major cities. A culture of complacency and "so what" was dragging the overall business down. It wasn't everyone. A very small group had been bullying—for lack of a better word—the team and creating an environment of social decay and fear. Employee churn was very high. Discussions with the instigators of the crappy culture about where the business needed to go in order to become sustainable and thriving again were met with resistance and significant negativity. I found it mind-boggling that they were completely convinced I would not shut the business down and the "union" would protect them. Equally mind-boggling was their belief that I would simply give up and go away like so many leaders before me. The ringleader in the group was even the local shop steward for the union.

It would have been easy to build a culpable case against the problem children and terminate them. However, that would have only made them into martyrs in the other employees' eyes. The solution was to create a warm, caring, open, and honest environment. We did this by putting a coat of new paint on the place, occasionally serving the frontline team coffee and muffins at their desks, working to build relationships with all, holding open meetings with everyone to cover all the 24/7 shifts, answering any questions they might have, involving as many as possible in strategy discussions, and forming teams to drive change. The plan was to turn the team's positive energy against the cancer that was decaying the business.

The cancerous team members did their very best to resist every initiative, including filing one grievance after another. They put all their energy into occupying my every waking moment. Still, along with an awesome team of managers, I persisted.

I moved my office onto the floor of the biggest problem location. I purposely kept it open—never locking the door or my desk when I left for the evening or to travel somewhere. One morning when I came back to the building, my office had been destroyed. Prized pictures were broken, drawers overturned, papers everywhere. The criminal act would have been easy to prosecute since security cameras would have caught the ringleader doing the destruction. But without saying anything, I began to clean up. After an hour of clean up, I had my office put back together.

The next morning, I found the same thing. Destruction. My office was once again a mess. Again, I simply rolled up my sleeves and started to put it back together—in essence, removing the graffiti. An amazing thing happened that second morning. Employees, walking by on their way to their morning break, stopped at my office, came in, and started helping me clean up. A stronger message could not have been made that they were tired of the bullying and the environment of fear they were working in. The word soon spread. I never had my office vandalized again.

Team members started participating in my planning and strategy sessions. They suggested ideas for improvements to culture, customer service, and performance. The problem employee who had worked so hard at bullying the team for years did his very best to slow things down; however, momentum eventually took over and he completely lost his power base. He quietly shrank into the background—never to be a problem again. The business started to flourish, and with that success, an engaged team was created whose members brought their hearts and minds to work every day.

As a leader, once you have unlocked the code to a great culture, your team will tell you that the front door to the office doesn't weigh as much as it used to. In other words, they enjoy coming to work. When that happens, customers win, the business wins, and the employees prosper.

As a leader, you have an obligation to the team, the customers, and the shareholders to create the very best culture. Your culture has to be a living example of your vision, mission, and values. You have an obligation to eradicate corporate graffiti the instant you come across it through leading by example.

Graffiti comes in all forms. From brand violations to messy office space, from inconsistent customer service to poor employee practices and procedures, and to leadership apathy. It's your job as a leader to do everything within your power to ensure graffiti is removed immediately when it appears.

As Gandhi once said, *"Be the change you want to see."*

What graffiti exists in your business?

How are you going to remove it?

CHAPTER 19

Meetings—And Other Complete Wastes of Time

"Half the time men think they are talking business, they are wasting time." — Edgar Watson Howe

Meetings, in most organizations, equal ARGH!!! A lot of meetings means very little ever gets done. And why is it that meetings are always scheduled for one hour? Especially when nothing actually gets accomplished until the last ten minutes—as if people wake up from their boredom-induced comas, after looking at their watches, and think, "Oh crap, time is almost up. We better get something done!"

Most meetings have no agenda, no objective, no real leader, no action register, no minutes, and no real outcome. What a waste of time!

It doesn't matter what level or role you have in an organization; you can be the one who finally stops the insanity and takes charge by asking some solid, non-threatening questions at the beginning of every meeting like:

1. What is our objective today?
2. Is anyone taking minutes for follow-up, or would you like me to?
3. How are we going to stay on track today?

You will be asking the questions everyone in the room wants to have answered. You will be seen as someone who cares about the subject and everyone's time—which is good for your brand. If someone takes offence to you asking those simple questions, you might want to re-think if you want to work for a company that has no focus, or probably doesn't execute very well.

When you get into a higher-level leadership position, you can start repaying people in your organization by showing how much you respect their time and doing some of the following:

1. Schedule meetings for only thirty minutes. WestJet Airlines in Canada has an executive meeting policy that states, "If a problem can't be solved in thirty minutes, then you are wasting time."
2. Take all the chairs out of the meeting room. It's amazing. When people cannot sit down and get comfortable for their afternoon nap, they will pay attention and want the meeting to be over quickly.
3. I run weekly "Huddle Meetings" in a common open area, among cubicles or in lunchrooms, rather than in a quiet comfortable boardroom. Once again, it's amazing how fast and productive the meetings are! I keep everyone at the huddle focused by keeping it moving fast. Each person only has a few minutes to give his or her update—just like in professional football where the team comes

together for a meeting on the field to discuss the next strategic play. Football huddles have an objective, a leader, and an action plan. And they last for about ten seconds!

4. Always, always have an objective for the meeting with a stated expected outcome. Someone needs to be the moderator who keeps everyone on track and away from side discussions. There needs to be an action plan from the decisions made. There need to be clear responsibilities and accountabilities assigned with due dates (otherwise, another meeting will happen).

5. Technology like smart phones and laptops are banned from the meeting. Period. If someone is doing email or texting, he is wasting everyone else's time. The offending party is also saying, "I am too important for this meeting." If it is important enough to have the meeting and the people there, then get it done without distractions!

6. Respect junior people in the company! Junior leaders who are asked to come to a meeting with senior people to present an idea, process, finding, etc., prepare themselves for days. They are usually so nervous that they cannot sleep the night before. Imagine how they feel when they walk into a meeting with the "Big Wigs" and see them behaving like spoiled kids in a candy store! Senior leaders should not be ignoring the presentation, having side conversations, shooting down the ideas presented like they were Julius Caesar in the Coliseum! Senior leaders and executives behaving badly in meetings are a major cause of culture decay! When executives take opportunities to show everyone how smart they are, they just prove how little emotional intelligence they have. Show your people at every level that they are incredibly important to the business by giving them the full attention and respect they deserve. Thank them for being there and sharing. If they have made some mistakes in their presentation, ensure that their manager gives them the appropriate coaching in order to help them grow and develop.

7. Show up on time! Being late is not only incredibly disrespectful to everyone in the meeting, but it wastes precious time and erodes your personal brand.

Email. Technology was supposed to set us free. Instead, being "connected" has made us lose our focus and given everyone the opportunity to hide behind technology. I worked in an organization where I witnessed executives emailing each other from across the room because, although both had Mensa IQ's, they lacked enough social intelligence to talk to each other. Imagine being a follower of these two leaders.

Email can be an amazing tool or a set of handcuffs and shackles. It's your choice. Here are some tips for leaders so they can make technology a time-saving liberator:

1. Schedule time each day for email. An hour in the morning and another hour in the late afternoon. If you are too available and are responding instantly, you will not get any real leadership work done. And remember, leadership is all about getting things done and through an engaged team of people. Your people will not be engaged if all they get from you is a task list from your email.

2. Set a minimum amount of time during off hours when you are available via email. When you are done with your scheduled time, turn the laptop off! Otherwise, it will call for you like a mistress in the night. You will find yourself wearing a trail in the carpet at home going back and forth to your email.

3. Do not sleep with your mobile phone in the same room! Put it on charge somewhere in the house where you will not be distracted by it. (See Chapter 30 "Home Is Not Where You Go When You Are Tired of Being Nice to People.")

4. Handle email once. Read it. Action it. File it.

5. Set up file folders where it is easy to find emails later if need be.

6. Your email inbox should be empty at the end of every day. If it isn't, you are not following Step 4 above.

7. Stop "CC'ing" unnecessary people. What a waste of time. I don't even read most emails when my name is in the "CC" field.

8. Keep it short. I love Twitter because you get 142 characters to say what you have to say. Brilliant! Long-winded emails may show how smart you are, but they rarely get read!

Co-Workers. Colleagues at work can be a massive waste of time if...

- You are going for a coffee with them every day at the same time and the same place.

- You are in Sales and you find yourself having regular lunches with other salespeople in your company. You will soon discover that you and your colleagues are the bottom-performing salespeople.

- You are participating in office gossip. Passive-aggressive behaviour is the surest way to short-circuit your leadership aspirations! Shake it up by starting to spread rumours about how good people are! "Did you hear about Rick? He is really amazing! He presented the most ingenious idea the other day!" Soon, people will not want to share their juicy trash with you because you won't be any backstabbing fun anymore! And, this is the cool part: you will have more time on your hands to get things done!

- You are receiving from your colleagues WAY too many forwarded email jokes and funny videos. When you don't forward or reply to these massive time-wasters, people will soon stop including you on the distribution.

- You reply in-depth to an email query from a co-worker. By simply replying with a couple of words or no more than one line, people will get the message that you are busy.

The best phrase in the business world for getting away from distracting co-workers is simply to say, "Well, I have to get back to work." You will discover that the whole gossip session instantly ends and everyone goes back to his or her desk.

Below list five significant action steps you can take to reduce the amount of wasted time in your business:

1. _____

2. _____

3. _____

4. _____

5. _____

CHAPTER 20

Yoda was Right—There is No "Try"; Only "Do" or "Do Not"

"I would rather die of thirst than drink from the cup of mediocrity."
— Stella Artois 1920s advertising slogan

Are we inspiring mediocrity at work? In this chapter, I will point out what is wrong with four little words that, if tolerated, will destroy high performance and inspire mediocrity.

To illustrate, let's begin with my favorite scene in the Star Wars' film *The Empire Strikes Back*. Poor Luke is down and out and attempting to throw a "pity party" for himself. It is evening in the swamp on some far off planet and he has landed his spacecraft there to seek the advice and wisdom of Yoda. Yoda is listening patiently to Luke's whining about all the things that are going wrong, and how Luke has been "trying" so hard!

Yoda finally speaks by saying, "There is only do and not do. There is no try."

No truer words were ever written into a script.

Your job as a leader is to build an engaged culture with the team around you. A culture of high performance and a culture of winning. In these nirvana business cultures, there is only do and not do. In these cultures, winning is celebrated and losing is equally celebrated. Winning puts revenue in the bank, high levels of productivity into action, builds higher levels of customer satisfaction, and reduces unnecessary costs. Celebrating losing means you are acknowledging that the business is learning, growing, adapting, and nurturing risk-taking.

"Trying" is, as Kit Grant puts it very eloquently, just a convenient excuse for not getting things done!

Whenever the word "try" or "trying" comes up in a conversation when I am in the room, I quickly interrupt the speaker to ask, "Why don't we stop trying and just do or not do?" The first few times this happened, people always looked at me like I was the most unsympathetic person on the planet. I am unapologetic. I explain that I would rather have a team of people who work four ferocious hours a day at doing and winning or losing than someone who puts in twelve hours trying.

Trying breeds politics, apathy, and mediocrity—Ouch! In business, the word "try" should be removed from the dictionary.

Another word rampant in mediocre cultures is "can't."

"We can't do that. We tried that in '65. Didn't work then, and it won't work now." I see teams in mediocre cultures sitting around meeting rooms for hours on end specializing in shooting holes in each other's creativity. I have even seen guys pulling out an imaginary six-shooter, pointing a finger upwards at their lips, and blowing away the imaginary smoke from the gun barrel after they bring down an idea faster than a duel in the O.K. Corral, occasionally even "high-fiving" the guy sitting in the next chair. Winning, high performance cultures are doomed with "Can't Cowboys" at the table. As a leader, your job is to get the cowboys on board or out the door.

"Can't" really means that the organization has stopped looking for innovation. It means that it does not want to grow. And, it means that original thoughts have all been used up.

Your job is to pull out the "Magic Question," and after reminding the team that "can't" doesn't live here anymore, ask, "What does good look like?" At first, you will get some objections, disguised as more reasons why it won't work. Acknowledge people's insights and ask again what would work? Keep asking, "What else would good look like?" You will soon get your team members to switch their thinking from "can't" to "can."

Steve Jobs at Apple was famous for throwing out seemingly impossible challenges. In the '80s, it was, "This new desktop computer has to fit in a box that someone can carry out of a store." In the early 2000s, it was, "I want my favorite music to be three clicks away." His engineers would always say, "It can't be done." And Steve would always reply, "It can. Figure it out." Occasionally, he would have to say, "Find a way to make it work, or I will find a team that will." Drastic leadership yes, but it was effective. And look at Apple today!

"Can't" kills innovation and creativity! In business, the word "can't" should be removed from the dictionary.

I go crazy in the office when I hear "hope." Hope is not a management tool. It really means; "We have no idea what is going on and we are hoping it all works out."

Leaders always have a clear idea of what good looks like and how they are going to get there. Their team knows what each individual is responsible for and what their individual role is. Leaders know whose action it is, when it is due, and how the action is going to be measured. Leaders actively follow up on actions and projects. (I learned a long time ago that what interests the leader, fascinates the team.) Leaders have clearly, and with passion, communicated what is going to be achieved, how, and why to every stakeholder who needs to know. And they re-communicate on a regular basis.

When you lead with purpose and a replicable structure, "hope" is eradicated and replaced with confidence and competence.

Likewise, in business, the word "hope" should be removed from the dictionary.

"If" drives me crazy! It is impossible to move someone forward when they are stuck in "if." "If" is a convenient excuse to hang onto the past and not move forward. "If only I had gone to grad school...." "If only I were taller (one I used to use)...." If only I'd had a different childhood...."

Get over it! Move on! Write all your "ifs" onto a rock and throw it into the river and then, never, ever look back again! Living your life in the past won't get you to where you want to go.

The word "if" should be removed from the dictionary.

Challenge: Start to pay attention to the words you use. When you catch yourself using limiting language or negative self-talk, turn it around with language that will move you forward.

CHAPTER 21

Don't Be Fooled by "Experts"

"All of us are experts at practicing virtue from a distance."
— Theodore Hesburgh

As a young groundbreaker who is growing, developing, and figuring out your way as a leader running a business, you will discover there is absolutely no shortage of people with ideas on how things should be and what you should do, or should I say, what you should not do. I call these people "experts."

Experts specialize in short-circuiting:

- Creativity
- Innovation
- Solutions
- Simplicity
- Change

They are the ones who major in pontificating all the reasons and things that won't work. They will sit in a meeting room, lying in wait for the opportunity to jump out like a leopard striking its prey, and point out to you all the obvious causes why they think something will not work. Their negativity reflexes are so well-refined that you may not even see them coming. Sometimes, they will dispense their advice and then turn to a fellow "Can't Cowboy" and proudly "high-five" him. "Did you see that Tom? I showed him!"

This is in line with a human behaviour that, unfortunately, the majority of business people display. It is far safer to dispense reasons for why something won't work than to participate in suggestions on how an idea can be implemented. Nobody ever got fired for suggesting reasons why something should not be tried. In their minds, a ship is much safer in a harbour than facing the dangers of exploring unchartered waters. They are perfectly happy where they are and want no part of anything that looks like it might require some work on their part.

I think that is so wrong! In fact, I think there should be a soccer referee in every meeting room. When the referee hears a participant point out why something won't work without immediately suggesting an alternative idea or solution, the person gets a "yellow card." If someone gets two yellow cards in the same meeting, he gets a "red card" and is sent off the field (without pay for the day, of course!). An immediate red card is given out if the participant shoots down an idea based on political reasons, or he is not in line with the values of the organization in dispensing his opinion. Accumulate three red cards and you are fired!

I wonder how quickly people would offer solutions to problems if their take-home pay were tied to it. I think an organization would probably triple its growth if it eliminated yellow card behaviour across the business!

Sometimes, the "experts" hide their advice behind a veil of data and analysis that makes it difficult to see that they are actually getting in your way. These guys should get a yellow card too, unless they can use the magic of their analysis and reams of data for good and not evil. The yellow card can be avoided if they can immediately show how the data indicates what might work instead.

As a leader, you need to become highly skilled at identifying "experts" who are not going to help you move forward. Let your vision and strategies be your guide. Use the solid reasoning that all problems can be solved. A focused team in the right environment can find ways to bridge gaps and move forward. There is no marketplace or competitive problem that cannot be mitigated.

Use the magic question, "What does good look like?" as your guide.

When Boeing was designing the 777 airliner, the vision was to break conventional paradigms and build an aircraft that was easy to maintain and was more reliable than any other airplane. They wanted the "triple-seven" to become the very first dual engine airliner certified to fly trans-continentally. Up until that time, a transcontinental airliner needed to have more than two engines.

The design vision was summed up in a very simple approach. The head designer once said to his designers that he wanted each and every door on the airplane to be interchangeable on any opening. This plan was groundbreaking—it had never been done before. Until that time, all doors were different sizes because of the different curvature of the fuselage. The design team came back multiple times, saying it could not be done and here were all the reasons…(yellow card behaviour). Finally, the head designer issued a red card warning: "Find a way to make it work or find another job." The team found a way.

The Boeing 777 smashed paradigms and became the model that today most aircraft are designed around. Because of the innovation that went into the design, the plane was certified to fly transcontinental, and all other twin-engine jets soon followed in its footprints as other aircraft companies upgraded their designs to fly across the oceans as well.

Remember, there was no end to the line-up of people waiting to tell Christopher Columbus he was crazy to sail over the horizon.

> How will you get the "Can't Cowboys" in your world onboard? (Remember, if they won't get onboard, you need to get rid of them—always surround yourself with people who are positive and authentic.)

CHAPTER 22

Flight Simulator

"A man that does not think and plan ahead will find trouble
right at his door." — Confucius

Pilots train countless hours for what, in all likelihood, will never happen. Thankfully! Their level of training and dedication makes the air the safest place to travel from one place to another. They spend most of those hours of training inside a simulator—a magical box that replicates the cockpit environment and allows computers to replicate disastrous scenarios that test a pilot's decision-making and management abilities. The flight simulator pushes the boundaries of reasonableness and allows pilots to learn the skills of trusting their equipment, training, processes, intuition, and innovation without the loss of life or a multi-million dollar aircraft.

The law enforcement world has simulators now as well. They consist of a computer-driven three-dimensional or virtual world that they can immerse themselves into to test their reactions and decision-making abilities. They are able to walk into dangerous looking environments and make split-second decisions on perceived threats or harmless, innocent law-abiding citizens. Again, the benefit is no real loss of life and very valuable fine-tuning of skills and intuition!

In leadership, sadly, we do not have a simulator—an enclosed box we get to crawl inside so computers can throw bizarre situations at us to fine tune our abilities to deal with problems, ambiguity, people, and stress. Wouldn't it be great to run a set of computer-generated simulations where leaders could practice dealing with the announcement of a change in the business, how the market will respond to a message or product release, or how a meeting with board members, investors, customers, or potential partners could go? A device like that would sell millions of systems!

If I had access to a Leadership Simulator, I would have saved my businesses millions of dollars from marketing campaigns that were a disaster, business ideas that never got off the ground, threats from competitors, opportunities that went untried....The list goes on and on!

If only a device like that existed!

But then, why couldn't it? A mistake leaders make quite often is jumping blindly into a situation without conscious thought of the outcome. They enter the situation thinking that there can be only one outcome—the outcome that they want. Naïve thinking at its best!

Additionally, I see countless managers who analyze situations to death. Running "what if" scenarios to the point where nothing ever happens because they get analysis paralysis. Again, naivety at its other best.

The answer lies somewhere in the middle.

Great leaders understand that situations rarely turn out the way they imagine them in a nirvana world. They understand that an idea, change process, or negotiation outcome most often turns out somewhere between nirvana and disaster. And they avoid disaster by thinking about their desired outcome, their best alternative solution, and their "walk away" scenario.

Similar to what pilots go through in the simulator and their preflight checklists, great leaders understand that a winning situation or outcome is one where there are no clear winners if there is a loser. They understand that sometimes you have to walk away and rethink your position or solution. They understand that winning means both sides are happy with the outcome. They understand that there are solutions to every problem. And, they understand that if they explore all the options and opportunities beforehand, it is easier to mitigate emotions, threats, and disasters.

When I am about to go into an important meeting, negotiation, people problem, market problem, revenue, or cost crisis, I use my imaginary leadership flight simulator. I ask myself or my team whom I will be working with on the issue, "What is the best case scenario? What is the worst that can happen?" and "What is likely to happen?" We then explore possible outcomes by using the magic question. It is the best flight simulator a leader can have. Asking yourself, "What does good look like?" helps you develop desired outcomes to all the potential problems that could happen.

Exploring situations by following a replicable process helps you and your team to uncover strengths, weaknesses, opportunities, and threats, and to develop strategies for dealing with them. The process is invaluable for helping you to deal with stress and the unexpected.

For example, you and a colleague have finally secured a meeting with a very critical decision-maker on a contract your company has been working on for months. The decision-maker is vital to moving the business forward. You have thirty minutes of her time to review what has happened to date, position the win for the decision-maker's organization, and close the deal. What are some of the things that could play out, and how will you deal with them? Here are some examples:

- The decision-maker cancels or postpones the meeting while you are driving over to her office.
- She makes you wait in the lobby for fifteen minutes with no expectation of when the meeting will happen or whether you still have the thirty minutes that were scheduled.
- She unexpectedly has a team of hyper-analytical people from her business join the meeting.
- She announces that they need another four months to decide.
- She announces that their lawyer has a huge problem with the contract language.
- She announces that you have won the business, but you need to shave 30 percent off the price.
- She announces that she is going to award 50 percent of the business to you at the agreed to price and 50 percent to a competitor.
- Etcetera.

All of the above have happened to me in the past and were completely unexpected. And, this list could go on and on. But, with some discussion ahead of time with your team, you can brainstorm the most likely scenarios and what you can do about them before they happen.

In leadership, you cannot successfully fly by the seat of your pants, or in other words, fake your way through every scenario you come across. You might every once in awhile; however, you cannot on a lasting basis. You need to develop some form of leadership flight simulator that you can immerse yourself in to design the best-case solutions to complex problems. This process will enable you to respond quickly and naturally when something happens and…without stress.

Occasionally, something will still pop up that you had not anticipated. When that happens, fall back on your strategy and do not panic! Keeping your game together is crucial to your career and to the leadership of the team following you.

Think about some of the disasters you have had erupt in front of your eyes when you were busy pushing the boundaries of business.

What did you learn?

What would you do differently?

What would a leadership simulator exercise have done to help you manage the stress and potentially script a better outcome?

CHAPTER 23

Everyone Is in Sales—And Customer Service Too for that Matter

"Negotiating techniques do not work all that well with kids, because in the middle of a negotiation, they will say something completely unrelated such as, 'You know what? I have a belly button!' and completely throw you off guard." — Bo Bennett

Nothing happens in business without a sale. Nothing lasting happens in business without happy customers. If you forget everything else from business school or about being a leader, do not forget that!

You may be in finance, engineering, HR, or the warehouse and never have any interaction with sales or the customers. Yet, if you are not absolutely fanatical about supporting sales and obsessed with serving customers, you will not have a job.

Why? Well, if the first sixty years of the twentieth century were all about manufacturing and the next thirty years about distribution, and the last twenty about technology, from here on out, it is all about the customer. This is the age of the customer! Because of the flattening of the world by the Internet and social media, customers have access to power that can bring a company to its knees. The mindset has to shift, and I would say immediately, to make it easier than ever for sales to build deep consultative relationships with customers. The entire organization needs to understand that customer loyalty is more fragile than ever, and every process and system in the business has to be geared toward serving the customer—allowing him or her to get information and service easily, and when and where they want it.

As a leader, become obsessed, infatuated, and consumed with supporting sales and customer service. I have lost track of how many organizations I have been part of where I felt like I was pushing water uphill when it came to sales and customers. I guess I was ahead of my time, but the time has finally arrived! Your job in the future as a leader is going to be more about teaching the organization, from CEO to mailroom (if there still is a mailroom), to be fixated on customers versus processes and procedures that are designed for the company's comfort and convenience.

Forget loyalty programs and binding contracts. They just make it hard for customers to leave you. Is that what you want—a customer who feels like a hostage? Instead, obsess over value to customers and turn them into stark-raving apostles for your business who tweet, like, blog, video, and post all about you to everyone they know!

Gone are the leaders who think sales and customer service are for the VP of Sales. I worked with a CEO once who had a finance background; she spent all her time in her office going over data. She developed a massive mistrust for everyone in the organization (and actually said it out loud many times!)

because of the numbers she saw in front of her. If she had taken walks and worked to understand the pain the team was suffering because of her complete lack of strategy around serving customers, she would have been able to lead the right changes and motivate the team. Instead, she had record employee churn, resulting in decreasing customer satisfaction, and a loss of over a million customers, 15 percent revenue, the number one market position, and finally, her job.

Understanding your customers and your sales organization is paramount. And when I say sales organization, I mean everyone in the company. Making the shift from "departments" or "silos" to thinking everyone is in sales is a leap that will drive your leadership to the next level!

Get good at social listening. Today's social networks give you instant feedback about your products and services. I love it! As a marketer, I used to spend thousands of dollars and hours of time on focus groups and surveys, which took forever to get feedback on. When you are a great social listener, you know instantly where you need to replicate and what you need to change.

Get good at social engagement. When you know what customers care about, make it easy for them to engage with you socially. It will drive traffic to you! As a leader, you need to teach the organization that social marketing is not just a marketing thing or a weird department of kids somewhere in the building who waste their time tweeting all day—it is an organization-wide obsession.

More and more organizations are now seeing the benefit of allowing everyone in the company to interact socially with customers and prospects. The lines of delineation between sales, customer service, and the rest of the company just got really blurry! This new frontier has to be embraced by everyone, and you have to lead it, even if you are a leader of one!

If you are not in sales (by title), go over to the sales floor tomorrow. Don't wait—just do it! If your company has an inside sales team, grab a headset and "plug-in" on some customer calls. Really and truly get an understanding for the issues the sales team is confronting. What are the objections they are facing? How can you help? Bring donuts and coffee with you one day and go to every cubicle on the floor—spending time with each sales rep and serving him or her coffee. The experience will be powerful in terms of your understanding of customers, and a massive accelerator to your leadership stock price too! If you have an outside sales team, get out of the office and go for customer visits with a sales guy. Adopt a customer and help to build strategies and lead the removal of roadblocks for the account. Spend time with the sales leaders; brainstorm with them how, together, you can streamline processes and procedures.

I make it mandatory that every leader in any of my organizations spends time with sales and customer service teams on a regular basis. I love it when I first bring up the concept and I get these very weird looks of, "Are you smoking something? Me? You want me to sit down with a headset on and listen to sales or customer service calls?" But because position power has its privileges occasionally, I insist and even make it part of their objectives. The amazing part always comes right after they have had an hour listening in on calls; they come back to me like kids at Disneyland. They are excited beyond belief about what they have heard and learned, and more importantly, the cool ideas they have for making things better for the customers! I ask them about what good looks like; then listen to the ideas. We work through potential execution strategies. Then, happy with themselves, they turn and leave my office. I just smile. Another leader is on his or her way to getting it!

Challenge: Survey each person in your business, from the janitor and mailroom to the accountant and HR person. Ask them how their individual roles serve the customer, ask for their ideas to better serve the customer, and ask what they hear about the company on the street from customers. If they are clueless, meet with the employee individually to explain his or her role as a salesperson for the company and to brainstorm ways to enhance it.

CHAPTER 24

Who Got You Here?—Never Forget Your Roots

"There are two lasting bequests we can give our children: One is
roots, the other is wings." — Hodding Carter

I began my working life as a teenager washing dishes in a senior citizen home.
After high school, I was indentured as an apprentice electrician. After four
years of training, I was a full-fledged electrician—working with significantly
dangerous power systems in an industrial environment. I did not like it. I
learned some major things, though. I learned that I loved entrepreneurial
opportunities, and from that, I learned to serve customers. I learned what it
meant to be a frontline employee. I also learned how to work in a team. I am
forever grateful to the team I worked with and to those businesses' leaders for
the lessons in leadership and culture.

When I turned thirty and Colleen was finished with school and well-established as a nurse, I went back to night school to start my business education. My experience as an electrician, however, has served me all my life in terms of leadership and building great teams. Not a day goes by that I am not grateful.

What are you grateful for?

Following is a story of gratitude that I love! It is a poignant example of how the best leaders in business and in life realize they did not get to where they are on their own.

Who Packed Your Parachute?[1]
Author Unknown

Charles Plumb was a U.S. Navy jet pilot in Vietnam. After seventy-five combat missions, his plane was destroyed by a surface-to-air missile. Plumb ejected and parachuted into enemy hands. He was captured and spent six years in a communist Vietnamese prison. He survived the ordeal and now lectures on lessons learned from that experience!

One day, when Plumb and his wife were sitting in a restaurant, a man at another table came up and said, "You're Plumb! You flew jet fighters in Vietnam from the aircraft carrier Kitty Hawk. You were shot down!"

"How in the world did you know that?" asked Plumb.

"I packed your parachute," the man replied. Plumb gasped in surprise and gratitude. The man pumped his hand and said, "I guess it worked!"

---

[1]   http://www.agiftofinspiration.com.au/stories/attitude/parachute.shtml
Accessed December 20, 2011

Plumb assured him, "It sure did. If your chute hadn't worked, I wouldn't be here today."

Plumb couldn't sleep that night, thinking about that man. Plumb says, "I kept wondering what he had looked like in a Navy uniform: a white hat; a bib in the back; and bell-bottom trousers. I wondered how many times I might have seen him and not even said, 'Good morning, how are you?' or anything because, you see, I was a fighter pilot and he was just a sailor." Plumb thought of the many hours the sailor had spent at a long wooden table in the bowels of the ship, carefully weaving the shrouds and folding the silks of each chute, holding in his hands each time the fate of someone he didn't know.

Now, Plumb asks his audiences, "Who's packing your parachute?"

Everyone has someone who provides what he or she needs to make it through the day. Plumb also points out that he needed many kinds of parachutes when his plane was shot down over enemy territory—he needed his physical parachute, his mental parachute, his emotional parachute, and his spiritual parachute. He called on all these supports before reaching safety.

Sometimes in the daily challenges that life gives us, we miss what is really important. We may fail to say, "Hello," "Please," or "Thank you," congratulate someone on something wonderful that has happened to him or her, give a compliment, or just do something nice for no reason. As you go through this week, this month, this year, recognize people who pack your parachutes.

Powerful message. I love the story because it constantly reminds me of everyone in my life, past and present, who has been a key contributor to my success: my wife and children, teachers, coaches, mentors, bosses, friends, colleagues, strangers, etc. The list goes on and on! You never would have got to where you are today without others supporting you.

Always, without fail, take time to talk to people in the business. Ask them their names. Ask them what makes them most proud. Ask them what they would suggest to make the business better for customers and the entire team. You will get some information you already know; however, you will get some "gems" as well! The word will spread about your conversations and that you took the time to talk with people. That will increase the "stock price" of your brand as a leader, and most importantly, people on the team will go the extra mile for you when it is needed.

Two things I need you to do....

One: Make a list of all the people who have helped you in your life. You will be shocked by how long the list is. Make it really hit home and gather pictures of as many of your supporters as you can. Paste them onto a board, stand back, and be amazed! How many do you owe a simple debt of "Thank you" to?

Lastly, inspiration and support come from the most unlikely places. Canadian multi-billionaire Jimmy Pattison owns an empire that stretches across media, automotive, food processing and grocery chains, financial services, and the list goes on. Jimmy is in his mid-eighties now and still keeps a grueling twelve-hour day pace in the day-to-day running of his empire. What is most interesting, however, is that when Jimmy is out visiting one of his businesses (and he does it every day), he always stops to talk to frontline people to ask them how to improve the business. On one trip to a grocery store that is part of 100-store network, he stopped and talked to a guy cleaning the store floors. He asked the employee how he got the floors so clean. After the employee took the time to teach Jimmy the tactical steps to cleaning the floor the way he did, Jimmy took the idea to a management meeting where he had the same procedure implemented in every store in the country.

From whom are you missing inspiration and ideas from in your world?

Start to make it a habit to stop and talk with everyone in your business and discover the hidden gems of innovation and ideas out there!

CHAPTER 25

Microscopes & Megaphones, Mirrors & Windows

"When we long for life without difficulties, remind us that oaks grow strong in contrary winds and diamonds are made under pressure." — Peter Marshall

People are funny. They are fascinated by what others do. Curiously though, leaders for the most part are not tuned into this truth. Except, that is, for the ones who are tuned into their egos and the attention that comes with being a leader.

As a leader, you are dinner conversation. It's true—people in your organization talk about you at the dinner table with their significant others and families. "You won't believe what he did today..." is usually how it goes. In the office, the talk often turns to rumors. Some team members somehow think their "peer power position" grows by being able to share juicy gossip. You are completely naked on the leadership stage. You might as well have the Paparazzi chasing your every move.

You have seen this gossip before; you may even be part of the circle when you participate in discussions about your company's CEO or your boss, or discussing company decisions that have been made and the rationale for them, how unfair so and so is, or even just what the VP of Marketing had for lunch, or what time the VP of Sales came into the office. The list goes on and on. People's fascination with people in positions higher up the corporate ladder than them is rampant inside every company in the world.

You are not going to change this behavior without a major culture overhaul in the organization. But you can choose not to participate in it.

As a leader, you do need to be acutely aware of it. For as a leader, everything you say will be amplified as if you spoke through a megaphone, and everything you do will be scrutinized through the company microscope. Your team will know what time you come into the office and what time you leave. They will know how many times you go for toilet breaks. They will be able to recite when you left for lunch and when you came back. They may even know what you had for lunch. They will know if you are married or single, how many kids you have, where you live and what your dog's name is, what kind of car you drive, what you did on the weekend. They observe what you are wearing. They know if you are in a good or bad mood just by the way you walk.

I have heard stories about CEOs having people look through the windows at their family homes to see what their wives look like! Yes, pretty creepy, but it happens. The higher profile your position is or becomes, the more you are subject to weird attention from people.

The key to all of this is, first of all, not to let your ego get too inflated by the attention. Like the band Cold Play's song lyric, "I now sweep the streets I once owned," if you are ever no longer in a position of power or leadership, you quickly discover that the people who may once have been fascinated by your life, suddenly don't give you the time of day. I have always found it fascinating how many people drop their leaders like a bad smell when they fall from grace with the company and get fired or transferred to another role. The best thing you can do as a leader is, first of all, not to get involved in the gossip about other leaders in the company. Next is to realize that if it all changes for you as a leader in the organization, either by your exiting the company or moving to another position, the group of loyal supporters you had enjoyed will change as well because, even if you may have been the best leader the organization has ever had, most people are not strong enough in their convictions and emotional intelligence to remain loyal to you when the next leader shows up.

The survival or coping mechanism a leader needs to adopt is to realize, "You are dinner conversation." It's real, so deal with it and move on. Next…realize that your every move is analyzed, scrutinized, and editorialized. That too is very real so deal with it and use it for good and not evil. What I mean by that is, don't play into the gossip circus. Never use privileged information as a tool to show team members how "connected" you are—it will completely destroy your credibility and authenticity. When you know something that you cannot share at the time, simply tell people when you get pressured for an answer, "I cannot talk about that at this time." That's it; that's all. Your credibility as a leader will increase. When you can share information, do it clearly, simply, and without drama. Deal with facts, and never comment on rumors and speculation. Help people understand messages by focusing on the "what and why," and how they affect individuals and their jobs.

When you discover your peers sitting around the leadership water cooler (meeting room) and speculating on the next big corporate restructuring or on the CEO's decision to cancel the Christmas party, do yourself and your brand a huge favor and remind the group that it's a waste of time to hypothesize on gossip and rumors.

Windows and Mirrors. Your stock as a leader (and leadership stock is measured by how much people trust you and will follow you on a journey) goes up significantly when you practice two simple "leadership optics" habits. Look out the window when times are good and look in the mirror when things aren't going so well.

Why does this advice fit in this chapter? Remember, everything you say will be amplified as if you are speaking through a megaphone. Everything you do will be magnified as if you are being viewed through a microscope.

When you make sure your team gets the credit (looking out the window) when times are good, word of it will spread throughout the organization, your team will love you for it, and your leadership stock value increases.

When you make sure you rise up and take responsibility for things that are less than perfect (looking in the mirror), your team will appreciate you stepping up and not blaming them. They will go to war with you anytime when that happens. Your boss will appreciate you for not throwing him or her under the bus. You will be viewed as someone who takes responsibility—an almost dead trait in business today. By the way, I have never seen anyone get a prolonged beating from an executive when he has stood up and done the right thing by taking responsibility. I have also never seen anyone get fired for doing the right thing—and if someone were to get fired for doing the right thing, he probably should not be working for a firm that doesn't value honesty and integrity.

When you appreciate megaphones and microscopes on the leadership stage, it makes you more strategic and better able to deal with ambiguity. Mirrors and windows are all about doing the right thing for people.

Have you given your team credit lately?

What do you need to give them credit for that perhaps you haven't?

CHAPTER 26

Teenagers—What They Can Teach You about Emotional Intelligence

"Silence is the element in which great things fashion themselves."
— Thomas Carlyle

If you are a parent of teenagers, you know of what I speak. If you have a younger sibling who is still a teenager, you also know of what I speak. If you have neither your own teenager nor have relatives with one whom you can spend time with, become a Big Brother or Big Sister or volunteer at a youth centre so you can get some valuable emotional intelligence training.

I have led thousands of people in my lifetime. At one point, I was even responsible for over 1,500 women performing stressful frontline work. When I was first asked to come into that business and do a turn-around, I arrived at my new office and met up with my new executive assistant. She quickly showed me around my office, including letting me know where she kept supplies in my desk. "And in this drawer," she said, "is where I keep your supply of tissues." "Tissues?" I replied. "What do I need those for?" She responded by saying, "Oh, you'll find out!" And within twenty-four hours, she was right. That day, I had two of my new managers in my office crying about something that was messed up in their lives. Oh my, it was quite the lesson in becoming a leader who could listen and not wade into solving problems—just listen. Especially when I had come from a service business populated with a couple of hundred macho male types who, when they got on my nerves, I could tell to grow up and go do their jobs.

Teenagers, though, are something completely different. Teenagers have had fourteen years of living with you. Studying your every move, your every mood. They know what buttons to push to get what they want. Fourteen years of analyzing strategy, reactions, and alternatives. You can become a brain surgeon in less time than a teenager has been sharpening his or her skills at managing you.

Teenagers don't get paid to follow your vision and strategies. In fact, their hormone-ravaged bodies are seemingly always on the lookout for a reason to debate with and test you over anything. And when they feel things are not going their way, they resort to psychological and emotional warfare. If that doesn't work, they engage the other spouse to help them. Living with a teenager is such a polar opposite from the workplace where everything is logical, structured, and practical.

Just when you think you have made headway in figuring out the teenager's mind, he or she will change the rules so any sense of normalcy you thought you were building is scrambled on the floor.

It is tiring. It can be frustrating. I think teenagers are why they invented red wine for parents.

The thing is, as a parent, you spend the early days of childhood teaching your son or daughter your value set and how to be a functional member of the family with routine and structure that is critical to the child's development. Small children rely on you for everything in Maslow's Hierarchy of Needs from basic safety to security and self-actualization. Your children listen. They adore you. They even brag about you to their teachers and friends. They emulate your every habit—good and bad. They are actually fun to be around! For twelve to fourteen years, this behavior is all you know as a parent.

Then one night, some force of nature called the "Puberty Fairy" sneaks into the angelic little children's bedrooms and sucks the brains from their bodies. For when they wake up the next morning, everything changes! They won't eat their favorite breakfasts. They want to wear weird clothing. They develop outrageous table manners. They argue about everything you suggest; for example, "What a beautiful day it is outside!" is responded to by the alien now inhabiting your teenager's body with "It's ugly outside!" And they do not want to be seen with you! So begins six years of unconditionally loving an alien being who only wants you when in need of money or a ride somewhere.

Why is being around a teenager an important lesson for you as a leader? Simple. Unlike dysfunctional employees, you cannot fire your teenager. But, as with employee relations, where you want to develop a happy and engaged team that serves your customers beyond expectations, you need to have harmony at home. Having your ego bruised daily is good for you. Having to negotiate every aspect of everything that your teenagers now think they control—like the television, the bathroom, and the kitchen—is good for you. Learning how to have a civilized conversation with someone you could easily outwit and overpower with your logic is good for you. Learning how to get information out of someone who only replies, "I don't know" to your every question, is, again, good for you. A teenager will teach you all you ever wanted to know about your hot buttons because they know just what buttons to push and the most inappropriate times to push them for you. This education about your emotional buttons is incredibly good for you! Learning how to keep your composure and your cool when all you want to do is reach across the table and put your hands firmly around their little necks is, yes, very good for you!

And, just when you think you have built up this impenetrable defence from your teenagers taking all the wind out of your sails, they will have a personal crisis and immediately turn to you to solve the problem. They will tell you how they appreciate you and how you are the best parent ever! You feel needed again, so you instantaneously put on your superhero outfit that you loved to wear when they were little children. Quick as a flash, you solve the crisis and tell yourself that from now on, the house will be in harmony again like it used to be. Wrong! Crisis averted, but your teenager is back, still uttering single syllable words and upsetting the balance in the house!

Learning how to deal with all aspects of living with a teenager teaches you that every other problem at work is so very easy. Teenagers must be a key reason why you rarely see senior leaders get upset or lose their tempers at work. They probably have teenagers and they have seen it all. They have learned that you get much farther in a crisis by listening, gathering information, and then calmly laying out a strategy to correct the course of the organization again. They always refer to distractions in the context of, "Is this part of our strategy or a distraction?" If it is the latter, they lead the team to ignore the distraction. If the issue can help the organization's strategy, they help the team understand how it will help and where it fits in the grand scheme of priorities.

I have learned that arguing with a teenager is pointless. Almost every adult on the planet could out-reason a teenager and do it while having a coffee and reading a book simultaneously.

From co-habiting with my teenage children, what I have learned about emotional intelligence that can be applied directly to leadership in business is to:

1. **Listen**. Stephen Covey says to "Seek first to understand; then be understood." He said that because he had teenagers. Especially when your teenager is in a talking mood, which is rare, just shut up and listen. Learning how to listen and not talk is the very best leadership skill you can learn.

2. **When it is your turn to talk, ask good questions** that are not emotionally charged. Like a good sales call, ask only "what" and "how" questions. Like, "What does good look like?" What do you want me to do?" What would you do in that situation?" When you ask questions that make it appear to teenagers that you value their opinions, judgment, and intelligence, they will surprise you by showing you that they really are intelligent!

3. **Focus on behaviours.** Remember, a teenager's self-esteem is more fragile than fine crystal. Even if their ideas seem way beyond rational, it is their behaviour that is out of line, not them. Like great interpersonal leadership, you have to make it all about the behaviour and not the person.

4. **Keep drama out of the equation**. Super critical! A teenager's life is full of self-imposed drama. The worst thing you can do is add to it with your own drama. Employees and teenagers need a leader who is calm in a crisis and always, without fail, links back to the vision, strategies, purpose, and values. Drama in the workplace by the leader never solves a problem or achieves long-term engagement.

What are your emotional "hot buttons" that cause you to react or behave out of character? What makes you feel angry, frustrated, or unappreciated?

What are the triggers?

How can you recognize the signs?

What can you do to deal with those "hot buttons" in a way that aligns with your brand?

CHAPTER 27

Learn to Speak—Do It Often and Have Fun Doing It!

"Man's mind stretched to a new idea never goes back to its original dimensions." — Oliver Wendell Holmes Jr.

The world's greatest leaders, alive or dead, despite coming from disparate cultures, backgrounds, economic conditions, religions, social status, genders, age groups, etc., have one thing in common: The ability to speak. The ability to speak in meetings, on the factory floor, in front of the board, on a stage, or in front of a client. They can, with conviction and passion, deliver a message or idea that moves people to do something different. Something people most likely would not do on their own. It is that leader's ability to convey a thought, a vision, a purpose, that inspires people to go far beyond what their own imaginations thought impossible.

Speaking is a key essence that great leaders possess over intelligent managers. And remember, I believe managers are to be found everywhere—leaders who have developed their leadership DNA are rare and…leaders have no shelf-life. Managers are replaceable.

I remember standing up at my own wedding some twenty-seven years ago to deliver the customary speech at weddings in Canada where the groom thanks his new in-laws for the gift of his bride. Our wedding was average in size with some 120 guests. I knew everybody in the reception hall. It was a happy day for me because I was starting what has turned out to be an amazing adventure with my wife, Colleen, and our family. You would think that this speech would have been an easy one for me to give. I was a wreck! I was so incredibly nervous that my voice was cracking, my mouth was dry, sweat gushed out of every pore in my body, my hands were shaking, and my knees were rattling! After my brief sixty seconds in the spotlight (which felt like a torturous eternity!), I sat down, completely spent.

I vowed at that moment never again to feel that out of control.

It has taken twenty-plus years of studying other speakers, practicing, taking courses, practicing, getting coaching, and practicing some more to get to where I am today. Today, I am able to take stage in front of thousands of people and speak with the audience as if I were having a casual conversation with a trusted friend over a beer on a Friday night. I feel completely at ease on a stage or in front of hostile union reps, upset employees, concerned board members, or a team I want to lead to a new vision.

Following are ten quick tips for getting good at public speaking. And, by the way, I consider public speaking any time you have to open your mouth as a business or community leader….

1. **Understand what is in it for the audience.** Your message will never be received unless you structure and deliver your message in a way that resonates with the listener. Spend time to understand fully what good looks like to your listener. Every human on the planet has a "WIIFM" (What's In It For Me) that he or she is listening for. That is the way we are wired. We are always looking, or listening, for value that connects with us personally. Understanding your audience and talking to its needs, versus standing there and talking about what is in it for you, will disengage your audience members so they will start thinking about grocery lists and what they are going to do after work tonight.

2. **Always structure your message so it has a beginning, middle, and an end.** That is, an introduction that sets up why your message is important to your listeners, then the actual message, and finally, a wrap up or conclusion that moves people to action. It's critical as a leader to have structure to your communications because adult followers need to have a message delivered in a way they can process it to understand how it is important to them.

3. **Tell a Story.** Nothing hooks people like a story they can relate to. Stories help an audience visualize the message more clearly and lock in the value you have for them. Steven Jobs of Apple was a master storyteller. He injected mystery, intrigue, and imagination into his renowned speeches on new products and futuristic concepts—both on the stage at MacWorld and with engineers at the R&D centre. Try starting a dialogue at the next meeting by saying, "Imagine if we were able to get this product to market a month earlier. What would that mean to our organization? How would that drive your credibility as an innovator and someone who gets things done?

4. **"Be brief and be seated."** (Winston Churchill) Say what you have to say and sit down. Especially true in a meeting or boardroom. I have met so many executives who just love to hear the sound of

their own voices. One I worked for used to have diatribes that went on for hours about himself. What was worse was that no one was allowed to leave the room when he was speaking!

5. **In a meeting, hook other participants by repeating thoughts and ideas they have had back to them.** Nothing gets people onto your page faster than knowing you have been listening to them. "Let me just quickly replay what I think you have just said to me…" It is a huge motivator to other participants to know you have been listening to them. It shows you care. When you show sincerity to others, they will repay you in kind.

6. **Get good with your voice.** Think back to the professors you had in college. Their monotone voices put the class in a coma faster than a sleeping pill. Your voice needs to be an integrated package with your body language and the story you have to tell. Your passion will be transmitted through your voice and body language. Watch actors on TV. Watch your friends and family when they are engaged in conversation. Their voices are not dull and boring. They are engaging, passionate, and energetic. Be conscious of your voice. How is it projecting? (Less than one percent of all speakers are too loud.) Does your voice have inflection? How is your speed? If you want to sell an idea or new direction as a leader, enthusiasm is a good place to start.

7. **Focus more on how you will deliver a message versus fancy PowerPoint slides.** I see countless managers putting all their effort into their slides—PowerPoint "decks" that have line after line of data, groovy graphics, and awe-inspiring transitions. Here is the big idea: Slides are not the presentation, you are! Spend about 20 percent of your presentation development time on building slides and 80 percent preparing for the actual presentation. Know who is going to be there. What are their "hot buttons"? What is in it for them? What will the room layout be? What does good look like

when you are completed? When you have all of that figured out, rehearse, rehearse, and rehearse! When you know your material inside and out, your brain is free to analyze reactions in the room. You can deal with distractions. You can stay in control of your nerves.

8. **Learn to read an audience.** It does not matter what country you are in or what language your listeners speak as their native tongue. Body language is universal. Learn to read an audience by reading their body language. By knowing that your audience understands your message (or not), you can adapt your presentation to engage to the maximum.

9. **Learn to recognize and control your nerves.** Everyone is nervous when present—on a stage or in a boardroom. Those who say they never get even a little bit nervous will lie about other things too. There are 118 known visible signs of nervousness that the human body will exhibit. You may suffer from some or many of them. When you are nervous before a presentation, pay attention to how the symptoms are manifested. Dry mouth, sweating, shaking, cracking voice, headache, racing heart, etc. When you know how your nervousness comes out, you can take steps to deal with it. Here is the key though: Nervousness can be controlled by three simple steps:

   • Know your material inside and out.
   • Have a simple routine to follow before you speak. Professional athletes and stage performers all follow a thorough pre-game routine, which is intended to get them focused. I listen to inspiring music. Some practice meditation, deep breathing, or do a physical workout. Discover your routine and stick to it.
   • Breathe! The number one mistake most people make when presenting or giving a speech is they forget to breathe. Irregular or shallow breathing causes us not to have enough critical

oxygen to think clearly. Oxygen deprivation affects our voice, making us more nervous. Practice taking two really deep breaths before you start a presentation. It will make a huge impact on your delivery, which will mitigate your nervousness greatly.

10. **Practice, Practice, Practice.** Remember, the majority of your audience would rather have you at the front of the room than themselves—even those with bigger titles on their business cards. Public speaking is your big chance to show the world what you have as a leader, and being able to speak with conviction and confidence is key to your career growth and development. Practice, make mistakes, learn, and do it again! One of the great speakers of today is U.S. President Barack Obama. Just for fun, search on the Internet for when he was the president of the Harvard Law Society, and you will discover an old video of him giving a speech to a group at Harvard. He was terrible! He is proof positive that great speakers are developed and not born! Get feedback from a trusted friend. Watch yourself on video. Get a coach. Whatever it is, just keep practicing!

Challenge: Have a friend record your next presentation with a smart phone. Watch the recording and take notes on what you need to improve. Focus on the delivery of the message and not how weird your voice sounds or that you think you look too short or too fat.

Build an action plan for what you need to improve. Get some coaching from someone you think is far better at speaking in public or giving presentations.

CHAPTER 28

Love the Place You Are In

"A pessimist finds the difficulty in every situation. An optimist finds the opportunity in every difficulty." — Winston Churchill

Our journey to leadership greatness, individual success, or a life that is by our own design, is full of twists and turns. Some of those turns take us closer to our goal, others are...puzzling. Puzzling because at that particular moment in time, you don't know how the situation fits into the plan you have for yourself.

A job that you hate. A boss who drives you crazy. One seemingly pointless scenario after another.

The key is in what you choose to do about it. You can choose to be unhappy. You can choose to move on. You can choose to learn from the situation. Whichever you choose is up to you. However, remember, life is far too short to choose a path that focuses on the negative.

The detrimental energy manifested when you choose negativity damages your brand, your relationships with friends and family, and most importantly, you!

Throughout my career, I have been approached by many people wanting me to mentor them. I love to teach and to give back, so I most often say, "Yes." Most people I mentor will come to an initial mentoring meeting with me and never come back. Is it because I am ruthless, cold, and mean? No, not at all. I am challenging for sure—always wanting people to realize their dreams, goals, ambitions, and true love in life. Most never come back because they discover that I am **not going to:**

- Wave a magic wand and give them the secret recipe to success.
- Say they don't need a plan for what they want in their lives.
- Let them get away without implementing their plan.
- Listen to them complain about how they hate their job, their boss, and their life.

There is no secret recipe. No magic wand or special water. The only secret is hard work.

You want to be successful? Work harder than anyone else. Period. Get up earlier. Work smarter, and keep developing yourself. Be ready for years of dedication, learning, hard work, and intense focus. Success rarely happens overnight and without effort. If you want greatness, you have to work at it.

Get a life plan and execute!

I am shocked by how many people hate the place they are in. And then they wonder why they are not moving ahead. The negative spiral of energy they emit influences every aspect of their lives. These are the same people who will leave a crappy situation only to find themselves in another one.

My advice? Love the place you are in. Learn to find the good in the job you have, the people you work with, and the boss you have. By all means, don't shorten your life and stay there too long. However, in the meantime, what can you learn from the situation? When you have the dream job, what will you as the leader replicate in your business, and what will you definitely not do?

Discover what every day, every situation, and everyone can teach you. If you think there is nothing you can learn, then lesson number one is learning how to open your eyes to opportunities. Over the years, I have been in some crappy jobs. And while I was waiting for a better opportunity, I chose to learn. I have learned:

- Volumes from the worst bosses on the planet
- How to stay positive and optimistic in the darkest of days and situations
- How to choose my responses to negativity
- How to lead my peers out of the depths of despair
- How to manage my manager

Values. Understanding your own personal values is paramount. Your core values are part of your DNA and have been adjusted or reinforced by your parents, siblings, friends, teachers, etc. Your values are the very foundation of your attitude. Your values will help you determine what you will hang around to learn from and when it is time to move on.

About ten years ago, I worked as an executive in a large telecommunications company. I worked there for a long time in various roles that taught me volumes about business and leadership. It also taught me how to learn from every situation and from everyone. And it taught me how important personal values are. After a significant change in leadership at the organization that saw close to one hundred vice presidents get fired, replaced, and the new ones eventually fired too, I was put in a situation where I was asked to do some leadership things that violated my values and would have had me treating people, my people, like consumable tools. So, instead of violating my values, I quit. And in quitting, as a long-serving executive, I walked away from good benefits, stock options, a great salary, and the significant six-figure severance package I would have received if I would have simply pushed back and got myself fired like all the other VP's who were rotating through the business. You can learn so much in crappy situations, but when your personal values are violated, it is time to leave. And in leaving, you will truly be better off in the long run.

You will have multiple bosses in your lifetime. Some will be amazing people—the kinds of bosses you would follow anywhere. Some, well, they are still a work in progress when it comes to nurturing the leaders within themselves. Regardless, there is something you can learn from all your bosses. The coolest thing I learned from my crappy bosses in my lifetime has been how to manage your manager. Not manipulate but manage. Every human on the planet has an internal self-focused need to understand "what's in it for me" in every situation. Even your manager. When you learn that everyone has this need and then you work to discover what each person's need is, then you have unlocked the secret to motivating people. Even your boss. Part of "loving the place you are in" is seeing the good in your manager. Learn how to manage "up" as well as "down." Discover what you can learn from your managers—after all, they did the job somehow.

What can you learn from your current place of employment or business venture?

What can you learn from your current boss?

What place is currently allowing you to teach yourself about your values, your attitude, and what you want to put into the life you are leading?

Do you have a life plan?

If not, ask yourself, "What would good look like?" and begin to develop one.

CHAPTER 29

Don't Drink the Ouzo—Work Internationally

"Teach us to walk the soft Earth as relatives to all that live there."
— Sioux Indian saying

Nothing in school (unless you have been schooled in an International Business School) prepares you for or gives you the valuable lessons as a leader or entrepreneur like working and living in another country—preferably a country on the other side of the world that is completely different culturally.

In 2004 when I moved my family across the planet to take on a turn-around project in Romania, I honestly thought I had some world-class leadership and business skills. Was I wrong!

The problem with being North American is that the business environment in Canada and the U.S. is, as the culture, blended and mosaic. Very focused and hard-working yes, but it truly is a blended and tolerant business environment that follows logical rules and basic norms.

In other countries, it is a completely different story. Most nations in the world have centuries of traditions, practices, and very defined cultures. I find it fascinating that the continent of Europe could geographically fit into the total landmass of Canada, yet Europe is made up of approximately fifty separate countries. You can drive through two or three different countries in one day. Yet in that drive, you will pass through completely different cultures. Cultures that have been protected by hundreds of years of families raising families and living no more than a town away from where their many greats-grandparents lived.

In Canada, it may take a person seven or eight hours to fly from one end of the nation to the other, passing through six different time zones along the way. Yet, the culture and make-up of the people and the way they conduct themselves is basically the same.

Within days of arriving for duty in Romania back in 2004, I was off on my first "road trip," hopping on a plane for a forty-five-minute flight to Athens. In Canada, the airplanes do not even get warmed up in forty-five minutes. Anyway, I was off to meet with our biggest reseller partner, whose head office was in Athens and who represented almost 30 percent of our total sales. We had regular quarterly meetings with our partner where we would review targets, incentive programs, marketing initiatives, and performance.

I arrived in Athens on a blistering hot summer afternoon. My team and I were met at the airport by Aris, one of our partners. He drove us to our hotel to check in and drop off our bags. Along the way, he introduced me to a whole new way of driving, with hand gestures and words I had never seen or heard before. Every once in awhile, he would point out some two thousand year old monument, and without skipping a beat, exuberantly share his opinions of other drivers who got into his way. All very comical.

We checked in at the hotel, changed into more comfortable clothes, and Aris then whisked us off on a tour of this amazing city. The finale was the Acropolis! Even more impressive than I had imagined! We spent almost two hours up on the Acropolis with our host giving us an up close and intimate tour. I had to pinch myself many times. It was surreal. A few days earlier, I had been in Vancouver where the oldest building in town was maybe a hundred years old. Now here I was standing in the middle of this engineering marvel that was over 2,500 years old.

Aris took us back to our hotel as the sun was setting so we could shower and chill-out for a few hours before dinner. Aris was back at 10 p.m. to take us out for dinner—in Canada, I am usually in bed by 10 p.m. We went to this magical beachfront seafood restaurant with the Regional VP and the General Manager for our partner's business. It was still sticky hot, but the soft breeze off the sea made it somewhat tolerable. Ouzo shots all around. Some Greek wine. More Ouzo. Finally at midnight, we looked at the menus and ordered. More Ouzo. Dinner finally arrived at one in the morning. The seafood was amazing, having just been caught that afternoon. I finally staggered into my hotel room at 3 a.m. and collapsed into bed.

Back up at 7 a.m. with a massively swollen head from the ouzo. Aris picked us up at 8 a.m. for the one-hour drive to the office. More synchronized driving acrobatics just to make sure no one fell asleep. We arrived at the head office and met up with the management team with whom we had had the amazing dinner the night before and into the early morning. They were all very friendly; I had never felt so welcomed and appreciated.

About 9:15 a.m., it was as if our host's schizophrenia medication wore off. Without warning, in unison the three of them started to yell and scream at my team and me. I was stunned! They went on for about five minutes about how they thought we were ripping them off, not giving them the support they needed, not advertising enough, allowing other partners to open shops too close to theirs, offering a commission program that was unachievable.... It went on and on. I was trying to get a word in, only to be cut off by another salvo. I thought, "What happened to our nice little evening we had? I thought we were such good friends!"

In the military, I believe they call this tactic, "shock and awe." I was shocked and in awe of how they could yell that loud for that long and apparently not breathe.

Just as I was starting to get a little agitated, but still keeping my Canadian calm and cool composure, their general manager, Dmitris, flipped open the briefcase he had on the table and pulled out a pack of cigarettes. Now, I am probably the world's biggest opponent of smoking so I had reached the point beyond agitated. I slammed my fist on the table and yelled out, "You are not smoking a cigarette in here!" Dmitris stopped, looked at me, and with a smile on his face, said, "That's okay. I will smoke a cigar." And he reached back into his briefcase and pulled out a cigar.

Beyond annoyed, I got up, grabbed my things, and walked out of the meeting room.

A few minutes later, my team found me in the restroom washing up. The first thing one of them said was, "That was good. I think we are going to get somewhere." Completely dumbfounded, I said "What?" The quick reply was, "This is how it goes. They yell, you yell, and eventually, we leave and go home."

"Unbelievable" was the only thing I could think. I was definitely not in Kansas anymore! Okay, I figured, I have teenagers at home; I can do this. And back into the belly of the Trojan Horse I went.

Back in the meeting room, Dmitris, Aris, and the regional VP, also called Dmitris, were all laughing. The head Dmitris said, "Good job, Canadian! We didn't think you had it in you!" And away we went for another eight hours. They yelled. I yelled back. I remember getting on the airplane that night and immediately ordering two drinks as soon as we were airborne. Back in Romania the next day, my boss called me into his office to ask me how it went. After I told him the whole sordid story, he burst out laughing. Puzzled, I asked, "What is so funny?" He says, "I just love the Greeks. It is always so entertaining!" All I could think was that I had had more fun getting a root canal. My boss, however, was very impressed that I had not made any concessions, telling me, "They will come at you harder next time until they find your breaking point." Oh joy!

I went on to discover that within the very small geographic world of Europe, the Turks, Hungarians, Austrians, Czechs, French, Italians, Germans, Irish, Dutch, Belgians, Bulgarians, and Portuguese all have completely different styles in business. They may speak English in business meetings, but that was the only similarity! After my Greek adventure, I soon started asking tons of questions and researching before every meeting with different nationalities. I bought a book called *Kiss, Bow, or Shake Hands: The Bestselling Guide to Doing Business in More than 60 Countries* by Terri Morrison and Wayne Conaway. It proved to be an invaluable resource for preparing to do business internationally.

Working and living in foreign countries is the best way a leader can hone his or her skills as a strategist and negotiator. You will become more conscious. You will find your abilities to deal with ambiguity and to keep your team focused on strategy will skyrocket. Most importantly, you will dramatically improve your ability to deal with drama and emotions in the workplace.

Find a way to get some international experience even if you have to work for next to no money. Oh, and one last thing…when you go out for dinner with business partners from foreign countries on their turf, don't drink the local beverage. It is all part of their strategy to throw you off your game!

Our world is very flat these days. If you have not worked physically in an international environment, what have you learned from working with different cultures via the telephone or email?

What do you do differently to work with each one, depending upon the culture or even the individual?

CHAPTER 30

Home is Not Where You Go When You Are Tired of Being Nice to People

"Never look down to test the ground before taking the next step; only he who keeps his eye on the far horizon will find the right road." — Dag Hammarskjold

This is a tough chapter to write. I am going to bare a bit of my early leader days that were very painful for me. One I want you to experience here so you do not have to live it for yourself because it is one of the worst things you can do as a leader. Do not make the mistake of thinking home is the place to go when you are tired of being nice to people.

Home is NOT the place to go and vent about everything that frustrates you in your job. Home is NOT the place you go to continue working like a dog doing email and reports. Home, or your personal life, is the reason you go to work, because it is work that finances your personal life. Home is also the place that will be there for you long after the job. The job—the business, you as a leader—is just the means to the end—not the other way around. Understanding this valuable truth is not being disloyal to your organization or your entrepreneurial dreams; it is what will keep you balanced, healthy, and strong to be better at what you do!

As a leader for many years, I get where you are coming from. I know the pressures you are under: revenue that is off plan, customer dissatisfaction, productivity numbers that are sliding. The union is not making your life any easier. The board is pushing back hard. The executive team is expecting more with less. Budget cuts again. Your team is feeling unmotivated and wants you to do something about it—maybe back off on targets or review salaries.

Yet, for you to be the leader you need to be so you can grow into your potential, maybe one day leading this company or another business, you need to create a very separate life away from the office—a life that has balance, love, and nurturing relationships.

Your family, your partner, and your friends usually have their own sets of issues; they may not care about your pain in the office. You have to accept that. Your partner may love you unconditionally; however, he or she needs to know you are there 100 percent to help build the other life you have together.

I spent my thirties working incredibly hard to build a career. Long, long hours in the office and on the road. Success in business was falling into place—mostly because I discovered halfway through my thirties the secret to making a plan and executing on it. But my home life suffered. I missed my kids growing up. I missed first words and first steps. My wife Colleen (what a saint) worked hard as a registered nurse by doing all her twelve-hour shifts at night so she could be home for the kids. She survived on next to no sleep. She held the house together. When we saw each other, which seemed like rarely, I remember being frustrated that she didn't have time for me. I was mired in this world of self-importance, which when I look back, was actually me feeling sorry for myself.

I felt sorry for myself because I was, in my mind, the only person on the planet who was working as hard as I was. And to top it off, no one was standing in line to give me gold stars for the self-inflicted hell I was starring in. I wanted balance. I wanted to run marathons again. I wanted to fly as a pilot more often. I wanted to experience the love I had with Colleen when we were first married. I wanted to be there and experience the joy of my kids growing up. Argh! It was frustrating!

But every morning, I would get up at the crack of dawn and head off to be a superstar performer in the office. Every night, I would get in the car and fight traffic all the way home and walk in the door expecting the idealistic life I was picturing, but somehow, it was eluding me. Why was I getting promotion after promotion at work and yet unable to get my act together at home?

The answer hit me like a toxic baseball bat one day. I was working with a consultant in the office on an employee project. She was an interesting individual. She was highly skilled in the area of employee engagement but a massive pain in the rear end for me. For some reason, she took every chance she could find to throw insults at me. Caustic ones. I tried to talk to her about how she was making it uncomfortable to work with her. She replied quite simply by saying, "Boohoo!" I complained to my boss about her attitude. My boss told me to "suck it up" because the project we were working on was getting great results. I thought, "Great! I have to pay for this over-priced consultant from my budget and need to suffer biting insults all day on top of it."

In hindsight, she somehow had a strange intuition into the personal pain I was putting myself through. One night as we were packing up for the day and I was getting ready to leave, without any context, she said to me, "Home is not the place to go to when you are tired of being nice to people." I replied, "What?" and she just walked out.

As I drove home that night, I kept replaying her words in my mind. What did she mean by that? Then it hit me. I spend all my days as a leader getting people at all levels to buy into a plan and execute to achieve successful results. It's exhausting! As a leader, you need to be selling to people all day long, every day. My drives home usually consisted of being on the phone for the whole hour talking to team members and customers. I would always arrive at my door, having just disconnected from the office about ten seconds earlier.

I was not switching gears from young leader and budding executive to husband, partner, friend, and father. Yet, when I drove back in the next morning and went for a run before starting work, I had at least two hours where I mentally prepared for being a leader again. I was failing to decompress from the day and get my head into my family.

My family was getting an up-tight, highly wired bundle of negative energy when I got home—they weren't experiencing the person they could look up to and rely on as an unconditionally loving part of their lives. I started a new regime of turning off my cell phone when I got in my car. I turned my sound system in the car on to listen to great music and inspiring tapes from respected leaders who talked about achieving balance.

This shift achieved a couple of things. First, it allowed me time to turn off work and focus on my wife and family. Secondly, it created another problem. After the first week, my wife asked me whether I had something to tell her. Confused, I asked her what she meant. She replied that I was being over-attentive to the kids and her, and she was wondering whether I was having an affair and feeling guilty about it. I told her, "Absolutely not!" I explained that

I was simply working hard at turning off work and leaving it "at the office." She then said, "Don't you be using any of that management stuff on me!"

This kind of attitude has always amazed me! Whenever I have gone to a management course to learn great concepts on leading people better, I would get back to the office or back home and everyone would be saying, "Oh, Bob's been on a course again!"

Argh! I was learning how to disconnect and decompress from the office, but I was still not getting anywhere! Colleen and I were no closer. My kids weren't running to the door when I walked in. The dog didn't even get up from in front of the fireplace. I was having the most amazing pity party.

One day back in the office with my nasty side-kick consultant, we were wrapping up another day. I was heading out the door when she lifted her head up after a long period of silence, and once again like some sort of psychic, she said, "If you want love, give love without expectations." I thought, "What a weirdo! She doesn't say anything to me beyond the project at hand all day, and then she blurts that out as I am leaving to go home!"

It was a quiet drive home that night. No relaxing music or motivational author. Just me and my thoughts. I kept replaying what she had said to me. As I got closer to home, I realized that my family had come to see me as this head down, tail up, workaholic they rarely saw, and they were probably hurting to be loved just as much as I was. Home is not the office. People aren't paid to follow your strategies and visions. Your family and friends willingly love you and want to be with you because of whom you are, not what you are! I vowed to be worthy of love by ensuring that I was first to love unconditionally. And that is what I did!

I can't remember when the change happened. But one day soon after, I noticed that I was having rich conversations at home again with my family. We were laughing. We were sitting together at the kitchen table long after we had finished eating—just talking and laughing. I felt like the weight of the world at work had been lifted off me because I had great relationships at home. Amazing how the two go hand-in-hand!

Colleen, bless her, booked a trip to Hawaii for just the two of us. I guess she thought I was worth saving as a husband. We had the most amazing time! Long walks, breath-taking sunsets, "Happy Hour" at a cool beach bar, and deep conversations about life and what we wanted to accomplish as a family. It was like a re-birth.

That was fourteen years ago. We have not missed going on a special trip at least once a year since. Even mini-escapes for one or two nights are a regular event. It has become a ritual and one of the best gifts we have ever given each other and our children because a loving husband and wife relationship pays huge dividends to a child's development and home-generated self-esteem.

I'll close off this chapter with these critical points:

1. Friends and family are where your trusted support network is—they will be there long after the job and the fancy title.
2. You're kidding yourself if you think the company and your team have the same loyalty to you as your family and friends. Only about 10 percent of the people you will work with will become part of your trusted friend group. The rest will, sadly, move on when you are no longer their boss or coworker. I have far too many colleagues in my network who put their careers in front of their families and ended up losing both!

3. Experiences live on way longer and are more precious than money and possessions. Like in the movie, start a "Bucket List" of things you want to experience and the people in your life you want to share them with, and then…make it happen now while you still have the good health to do it!

4. Develop a method for getting your head into the day ahead at work. This process includes going through visualization exercises just like pro-athletes do to prepare to respond to certain events.

5. More importantly, develop a process for decompressing between work and home. That does not mean going to the bar. It means developing a method of recognizing that work is over for the day, and it will be left behind as you shift to your personal life. Deep sea divers go through a process of decompression from their "water world" to the world on terra firma—you need to as well.

6. As the saying goes, no one on his deathbed ever said, "I wish I had spent more time at the office!"

What boundaries do you need to set between your home and your work life?

What strategy can you use to decompress before you go home?

CHAPTER 31

Become Conscious

"Remember a dead fish can float downstream but it takes a live
one to swim upstream." — W.C. Fields

Have you ever driven to the office in the morning, only to arrive at work and have the startling realization that you cannot remember driving through two of the busiest intersections along the way? Scary, isn't it? Or have you ever caught yourself thinking, "Oh, my gosh; where has this month gone?"

It happens. We get busy. Our heads are down and our tails are up working, organizing, paying bills, shopping, getting the kids to soccer, cutting the lawn, and then we collapse into bed only to do it all over again tomorrow. Forget date night! You just want to have thirty minutes all to yourself!

This experience is the human version of the hamster wheel. I can't say that it gets any easier. It can be more conscious though.

Think back to the first day of a new job, first dates, travelling to a far off and strange land. I guarantee that you remember each and every detail. The sights. The smells. The sounds. What the weather was doing. What it "felt like." That is being totally conscious. When you are in that state, all of your senses come alive and everything slows down.

You can have this state of consciousness every day. It takes discipline, but it is possible. Start right this very minute. Stop reading this book. Close your eyes and think about only what smells your brain is registering. Stop thinking about the grocery list! What sounds are you hearing? How does it feel to be in your body right this very minute? How do your clothes feel? Soak it all in.

Okay, now keep reading. Take this simple exercise to help grow your level of consciousness. Next time you see your partner or any significant other, drink in everything about him or her. What does he look like? Look for the good-ness in her that you fell in love with. Hug her and hold the hug long. Notice how she feels. How does her body feel when she breathes in and out? What does her hair smell like? How about the sound of her voice?

Warning. If you have been going through life in an unconscious, zombie state, your partner might think you have been smoking something if all of a sudden you start being conscious with him or her in your arms! Go slow. I have seen more relationships (including my own) grow into amazing connec-tions this way. Deeper loves and more powerful feelings than ever before. Yes, even more powerful than that teenage night in the backseat of your dad's car!

Start paying attention to the aroma of coffee. Fresh baked cookies and bread. The smell of the ground after a rain. Flowers. Mountain air. Freshly washed bedsheets. Shampoo in the shower. Consciously start to register it all.

Open your sense of touch to the feel of a newborn baby lying on your chest, the softness of a feather. I love to give my wife a back massage because I absolutely love to see whether I can feel each individual muscle in her shoulders—she gets a great massage and I get to be more conscious!

When was the last time you really tasted? If you are like most, you remember the first and last bites of a great meal or the first sip of an amazing wine. Everything in between is fuzzy because you stopped being conscious. I have a friend who is so much fun to have dinner with. She absolutely savors each and every single bite and sip of wine. It is amazing to have dinner with her because she brings the whole meal to life. Try it. Focus intensely on everything you put into your mouth for just one meal and see for yourself how the experience changes—how time slows down.

Cover your watch. Can you remember what is on the watch's 3, 6, 9, and 12 o'clock positions? Are there ordinary numbers, or lines, dots, or dashes? What is written on the face of the watch? If you missed any of these questions, start opening your eyes to colors, shapes, and textures. Burn the first image you see everyday into your mind and vow to pay attention to cool things that are virtually all around us. A blind friend of mine once told me she really didn't start seeing until she lost her eyesight. What she meant was that she finally became conscious. Try it yourself. Blindfold yourself at home for an hour and see how conscious you become.

When you connect again to your consciousness, life will slow down. Relationships will blossom. You will be happier, healthier, more generous with those around you, and more at peace.

Challenge: Spend thirty minutes focusing on being acutely aware of your five senses and the information they are collecting for you. Write down what you experience about the everyday world you are living in but are not noticing.

What are you smelling?

Hearing?

Feeling?

Seeing?

What does every bite of food taste like?

CHAPTER 32

You Have the Body of a World-Class Athlete—Being a Great Leader Starts Within You

"To keep the body in good health is a duty...otherwise we shall not be able to keep our mind strong and clear." — Buddha

This is absolutely the biggest personal mistake most business people, entrepreneurs, and leaders make. They treat their bodies like trash bins.

You would never buy a $100,000 racehorse and then allow it to skip breakfast, eat junk food, high fat/low protein meals, not drink enough water, drink too much caffeine and alcohol, smoke, not get enough sleep or exercise. Most people I know would not do that to a $5.00 dog.

If you think about the total cost of education and preparation that has gone into the *you* standing in front of a mirror, you are most definitely worth more than $100,000! In reality, factor in the future development and earning potential and responsibility in terms of leading other people's lives, and you are now a multi-million dollar asset.

A friend of mine's son is a professional athlete. As an athlete making well over a million dollars a year, his fitness and nutrition regime is not only very detailed and specific, but it is closely monitored by the team doctor and trainers. There is no room for flexibility or error.

As a business leader, you may think you do not make your living off your body, but you certainly make your living off your brain. And your brain is part of your body. Your brain is affected by the fuel you put into the machine, the rest that you give it, and the physical activity you put it through.

Okay, before we go any further, let's get all of the whining excuses out of the way for why you treat your body like a garbage can. Here is a list of my favorites:

- The kids kept me awake all night.
- I don't have time to have breakfast.
- I don't have time to plan out my nutrition for the day.
- I need coffee to keep me going.
- I need a chocolate bar in the middle of the afternoon to give me a boost.
- I don't have time to exercise.
- I travel so much—it's hard to eat right on the road.
- I need a drink at the end of the day.
- I am going to quit smoking in the New Year.
- I only need a few hours of sleep each night.
- I can't lose weight no matter what I do. It's genetics.

It is all a bunch a crap. You know that, so stop making excuses. Leaders do not make excuses.

I want to follow a leader who understands the value he provides and wants to operate at a peak performance level all the time. Would you follow you based on the lifestyle you have?

I can somewhat relate to where most people are when it comes to taking care of your number one asset (your body). I have been fit and healthy all my life when it comes to exercise. And I previously fooled myself into thinking that was enough. "Because I am a runner, I can eat whatever I want," I would reason with myself.

About ten years ago, my doctor discovered during a routine examination that I had a very high level of cholesterol. Because of genetics and family history, there was nothing I could do about it, he told me, so he put me on cholesterol medication. The medication made me feel terrible. It killed my energy and made my joints ache.

Next, I started doing really wild travel where I was flying across oceans multiple times per month. I was eating worse and not sleeping. I was a walking time bomb!

Out of desperation, I went to see a naturopathic doctor. She was horrified at my lifestyle and state of health. Between her and my amazing wife, Colleen, they put me onto a life-changing plan that has become my everyday habit.

The results? I am off of the cholesterol medication. My blood results are now that of a very fit twenty year old, including a low pulse rate and very low blood pressure. I sleep well. I look younger, and I have more energy and vitality than I have had since high school.

To save yourself the aggravation of poor health, lack of energy, and little ability to deal with stress, I'm going to give you some basic highlights of things you can do to live a healthier life.

I challenge you to work this plan for twenty-one days. I guarantee you will feel stronger, fitter, more energetic, and more in control. You will lose weight. People will start to comment on your energy and looks. You will get more results on the job. You will be way more focused.

This plan is based on *The Hormone Diet* by Dr. Natasha Turner, coupled with my personal experiences from applying many of these principles. I encourage you to read *The Hormone Diet* for more invaluable advice to improve your health.

Sleep. Sleep deprivation affects more than 70 million North Americans—That is a full quarter of the U.S. population! You need between 8 and 10 hours each night. Sleep is the most important factor in restoring hormones and keeping you balanced. A critical hormone that usually becomes totally unbalanced in most business leaders is "Cortisol," which is released to help us in stressful situations. Without rest, this hormone will stay out of balance and cause you to feel like you have no energy; it can cause weight gain in the form of belly fat. Getting enough sleep is critical to fat loss.

Sleep can be difficult when you are travelling—especially long-haul trips across multiple time zones. Taking a melatonin supplement an hour before you want to go to bed can help restore your normal sleep patterns faster. Melatonin is a natural supplement that your body produces to induce sleep. And, it is a powerful anti-oxidant!

To get a better night's sleep, try these tactics:

- Make your room as dark as possible.
- Limit the use of computers or watching of television just before bed.
- Keep your bedroom cool.
- Do not eat after 7:00 p.m. Having food in your stomach takes energy to digest and interferes with your sleep patterns.
- Wear very loose clothes, or even better, no clothes at all in bed! This allows your body to relax completely.
- Be in bed by 11:00 p.m. This is optimal for rebuilding your adrenal reserves.
- As soon as you can upon waking in the morning, open your blinds so the daylight helps your body wake up faster and more fully.
- See a naturopathic practitioner for more advice on getting a great night's sleep.

Exercise. Exercising is easier than you think. First of all, see your physician and get approval for an exercise plan. Being fit is paramount for peak performance. Exercise improves your energy, and it increases fat loss, hormone balance, strength, cognitive and emotional intelligence, your appearance, your ability to fight off viruses, and your capacity for handling stress.

If you are not sure about how to get started, invest in a personal trainer to set up a program custom-tailored for you.

- My weekly exercise plan is as follows:
- Two 45-minute strength training sessions
- Two 45 to 60-minute yoga sessions for flexibility and grounding.
- Two 45-minute cardio workouts per week. I will bump that up to four or five when I am training for a marathon.
- One full day-off from exercise. (This break is critical to body repair and helping to increase your metabolism.)

Diet. Okay, diet is the part where we all screw up and get lazy. Myself included. Believe me, though. Stick with a healthy eating regime for twenty-one days and you will not believe the difference in how you feel. Again, you should seek out the council of a naturopathic doctor for a custom plan for you and your health needs.

I will talk about the basics and then give you a sample of what an eating day looks like for me.

Travel can be challenging if you let it be. I have developed the habit of asking the waiter at restaurants to cook me the food I want and how I want it cooked (steamed, grilled, baked etc.). In some restaurants, the waiter will push back and say, "The chef will not cook it that way." To which I always reply, "The chef isn't eating it, is he? I am." Your body must be treated with the complete respect of the temple that it is. If a restaurant will not honor that, I always find another place to eat. I will not subject myself to something that is going to rob me or my customers of being able to perform at a peak level. I will also travel with a selection of protein bars, whey protein powder, and raw nuts for the times when I cannot get access to good food.

Your daily eating habit should look like this:

- It is absolutely critical to have three meals a day—breakfast, lunch, and dinner.
- Every meal should consist of equal calories from carbohydrates and proteins.
- Protein should be as lean as possible and be approximately the size of the palm of your hand.
- Eating at the same time each day will maximize fat burn.
- Do not eat after 7:00 p.m. I know the Europeans reading this will say, "Impossible!" Nothing is impossible. It is your body though.

- Have a mid-morning and mid-afternoon snack consisting of both carbohydrates and protein. I will give a sample of a snack further along.
- Drink lots of water. Drink most of your water between meals. Women should drink 2 to 3 liters per day, and men should drink 3 to 4 liters per day. Sugary drinks and juices do not count. Water is the best liquid you can put inside!
- No soda pop. Period. Not even diet pop (which is far worse!).
- Limit your coffee to one cup a day. Switch to green tea instead. You can drink as much green tea as you want and it is an amazing anti-oxidant!
- Alcohol. Limit yourself to two drinks per week. If you can, switch to red wine because the anti-oxidant values from red wine are fantastic!
- Avoid salt, sugar, white rice, food made from white flour. In other words, avoid anything "white."
- Avoid potatoes. Eat yams and sweet potatoes instead.
- Eat as many leafy green vegetables as you can. They help with fat burning and keeping the skin and other organs hydrated and functioning at their peak.
- It is good to have a "Cheat Day" once per week where you go off your plan and eat other foods. This once a week cheat day actually helps speed up your metabolism and limits the craving you might have from depriving yourself of your favorite foods.

Here is a sample of what one of my dietary days would look like:

Breakfast:

- **Water.** My first liter of water each day includes the juice of ½ a fresh lemon. Lemon is a powerful detoxifier.

- **Power Shake** consisting of ¾ cup of frozen blueberries, ¼ cup of frozen raspberries, half a banana, ¼ cup of fresh pineapple, ¾ cup of pure pomegranate juice (a powerful anti-oxidant), ½ cup of water, 2 tablespoons of ground flax seed, and a scoop of whey protein powder. I blend this all together and enjoy it! It has all the calories I need to get the day off to a rocking start and a balance of carbohydrates and protein.

Mid-Morning Snack:
- Two hard boiled eggs.
- The other half of my banana from breakfast.

Lunch:
- Grilled chicken.
- Salad or steamed vegetables. Salad would be dressed with balsamic vinegar and olive oil. No worries on how many steamed veggies you have.

Mid-Afternoon Snack:
- Apple.
- A handful of raw nuts (not roasted or salted) consisting of walnuts, pecans, almonds, and cashews. (These are a fantastic hormone balancers—especially for testosterone—and a great source of omega oils!)

Dinner:
- Lean protein—I try to stick to poultry or fish and limit beef or pork to once a week. For vegetarians, my experience is that you have a better grasp on nutrition than most people so stick with what works for you.
- ½ cup of baked yams or sweet potatoes or a ½ cup of brown rice.

- Three other vegetables like squash, broccoli, carrots, cauliflower, or beans. I avoid corn because of the high sugar content.

That's it. Simple, and after you get into the habit, it is very easy to do both at home and on the road.

Supplements. Because we cannot always eat as we should and because we have high stress jobs, I also take some simple supplements to help my body deal with stress. I take daily:

- A multi-vitamin (split into morning and dinner).
- 200 mg of Vitamin B Complex in the morning.
- 1,000 mg of Vitamin C (split into morning and dinner).
- 2,000 units of Vitamin D (split into morning and dinner).

Get yourself on a balanced, total body plan like this tomorrow! Today would be better. Do not procrastinate. You are most likely shortening your life with the lifestyle you have now. You may be young enough (you think) to handle it; however, once you get onto a cleaner living plan, you will discover how much energy you have been depriving yourself of enjoying.

It takes twenty-one days to form a new habit. Once formed, it becomes your new normal. Stand back and prepare to be amazed at your newfound energy and vitality!

> Challenge: Start now. Make a diary of what you eat and drink in a day and at what times. Diarize how you feel at certain times of the day (Example: tired, bored, hungry, frustrated, cannot concentrate, etc.). After a couple of days, look for patterns. I suggest that most of how we feel during the day is a result of how we fuel our body and brain.

Build a meal plan for yourself for the coming week on Saturday morning. Go to the grocery store and pick up everything you need. On Sunday evening, prepare what you can for the coming week and put it into labeled containers. Freeze or refrigerate to keep it safe. Work your nutrition plan for the week. You will usually start feeling more energy and a higher state of alertness within a couple of days! Stick to it!

CHAPTER 33

Run a Marathon or Something Else Really Stupid

"Only those who will risk going too far can possibly find out how far one can go." — T.S. Eliot

I have heard it said that, in order to be a successful leader, one must have courage, passion, initiative, and resolve. Most of us would say, "Yes, I have those qualities." To which I would reply, "How do you know?" As a leader, you never will know how far you can go, how much you have to give, and what you are truly capable of unless you go there.

I love to run. Running to me is one of those things I cannot wait to do. Picture a dog that knows it is about to go for a walk and you'll understand how I feel when I have running shoes on. Running to me is pure, unadulterated stress release, and a massive energy recharge combined with a chance to disconnect completely and think. I love to go out for a two hour run. I come back a completely different person.

A number of years ago, I got into running marathons. The thought was, "I love running. I love running for long periods of time. I am competitive. I might as well train for a marathon." I think, typical of most males, that was the extent of my thinking. What I discovered was that my competitive edge took over the pure joy of running. I started pushing myself in ways I had never done before. Longer. Faster. Harder. Hills. Speed sessions. Strength training. Getting up earlier. I became obsessed. Along the way, the joy came out of running a bit. But the edge within me kept me pushing harder and harder.

When I raced, I was even more obsessed, thinking only of the race in front of me and my strategy. I found myself actually doing a quick competitive analysis on all the other competitors—determining their potential strengths and weaknesses and then developing tactics for beating them. Developing strategies for my nutrition and hydration at certain times and distances. Playing with my weight. I probably should have been locked up in a sanatorium.

Training for a marathon is fascinating. Even though I have run and raced most of my life, nothing prepared me for the discipline and dedication required to run full marathons. It wasn't so much in the training. Yes, it required longer runs, which meant getting up way earlier than normal, being very conscious of balance in the training, special meals, ice baths after a long run, etc. But in a race, the pounding for 42 kilometers (26.2 miles), combined with the competitive atmosphere, really pushed my mental strength to the limits.

"Hitting the wall" as they say, at 30 to 34 kilometers is something hard to describe. One minute you are running along and everything is fine. The next moment, you are dealing with intense pain, no energy whatsoever, and emotional crashes. It is crushing, and the only thing that can get you to put one foot in front of the other and keep going is your mental toughness—the pure will to keep going. Of the seven marathons I have completed, I remember crossing the finish line of each of them a complete emotional mess, but feeling pure joy for having completed them, for the discipline I found to finish, and an unbelievable gratitude for my life and the loved ones I share it with. Physically, I have always been exhausted. And always, I have had the thought that I don't ever want to run again. Luckily, that particular feeling doesn't last long.

What keeps me going back and doing it all over again is the powerful feeling of having the determination to push through the obstacles and the pain. Running marathons and pushing myself through "the wall" has made me a much better leader. Not so much from the belief that the people who follow you are capable of so much more than they think they are (they really are), but because I know I am capable of so much more. That is really important on the road to becoming a world-class leader. When you know you are capable of more, capable of pushing through problems and challenges with confidence and conviction, your team will follow you.

Running may not be for you, and running a marathon is not for the faint of heart. Every time I run one, I think to myself, "Bob, are you stupid?" For most, training for a 10K or half-marathon achieves the same purpose. For some of you, pushing yourself to your limits, where you have to dig down deep for the resolve to finish, may not even be a physical challenge. It may be learning a new language, building a house, or going away all by yourself to a "silence wellness" retreat for a week. Whatever it is, find that something and do it. No other way can you discover how far you can possibly go.

Your leadership by example will inspire people to go on the journey with you. They will have more confidence that you have a plan. (You do have a plan, don't you?) After all, the root of leadership is "lead," not follow or give orders from a comfortable office somewhere away from the action.

Knowing that you, yourself, can deal effectively with change will make you a better change agent. And change is the biggest leadership challenge there is. Helping a team understand the what, why, when, where, and how of change is critical to being successful. When you have been to "the wall," you will know you can get through the change, and that frees you up to help the team get through the change too.

When have you hit the wall in your business or personal life?

Did you come out of it stronger?

What did that experience teach you that you now can (or already do) apply to your role as a leader and in life?

CHAPTER 34

School is Never Out—Just When You Thought You Had Learned It All

"Old age is compulsory, wisdom is optional." — Anonymous

Graduating from university, college, or business school is just the beginning. In fact, and sorry to burst the bubble, at that point, you haven't learned much at all.

To become a true leader whom people will follow, you have to take the theory from the classroom and get to work on honing your judgment and intuition. You need to develop emotional intelligence. You need to learn how to negotiate win-win outcomes with customers, employees, bosses, shareholders, partners, and vendors. You need to learn how to envision, focus, and execute. You have to get the experience that comes from watching others and doing it yourself. You need to learn when to pay attention to details and when to stay "high level." You have to make some horrendous mistakes, dust yourself off, and get back up.

If you are open to it and you check your ego at the front door, you will find the whole life-long learning experience can actually be fun. As I write this, I am fifty-two years old and have been a student of leadership for over thirty years, and I will be until my last day—or until my wife puts me in a nursing home where I will get three servings of soft food a day.

Of course, there has to be a Ten-Point List of things you can be working in your lifelong learning plan. Here's the one I have used for the past twenty years:

1. **Get a mentor.** Get more than one. A mentor can see things you are blind to. Similar to trying to watch a television program with your face pressed right up against the screen, you can't always see what's going on in your business or your own behaviors. A trusted mentor—one who has some battle scars, is aligned with your values, and will give it to you straight—is invaluable. You cannot buy that kind of education. Period.

   For some very strange reason, men are twice as likely to get a mentor as women. Come on, girls! Men are twice as likely. Really? This is the same gender that will drive around for two hours, refusing to stop and ask for directions, yet they will get mentors before women will?

   Look for a mentor who has achieved big things, pushed the boundaries, or led bigger opportunities than you have. Remember, you want to grow and stretch. Having a mentor who is equal to you in terms of achievement is pointless.

A great mentor is one with whom you feel comfortable enough to share your dreams, goals, and aspirations—someone who will not judge you, but who will push you hard when you show evidence that you are not executing. A great mentor will help connect you to other people who can help you achieve your goals. Learn from your mentor's mistakes; if he is any good, he will have had lots!

Be generous to your mentor(s). Make sure it is not a one-way relationship. Take them out for lunch and pay for their coffees. Remember, they are busy people and they could probably be out doing other things.

2. **Be a mentor.** I have had mentors most of my business and leadership life. It wasn't until I started mentoring others, however, that I discovered how much I could learn from teaching, coaching, and listening to my protégés. You have to listen intently and coach your protégés to execute on their plans and gently reprimand them when they consistently overpromise and under-deliver. In order to do that, you need to make absolutely certain you are advising them on a practice that you yourself follow. "Do as I say and not as I do" will not cut it when you are a mentor.

3. **Get a mastermind partner.** Mastermind partners are people you trust and respect. They are completely different from mentors because they are usually in the same place as you are. They are goal-driven and want to succeed.

The idea is to help each other. You share your goals with them, and they, in turn, share their goals with you. You meet on a regular basis and take turns sharing what you have accomplished on your plan. You gently nudge each other when you or they are off-plan, and occasionally, you give your partner realistic feedback about his or her lack of execution, motivation, or complaining.

Having a mastermind partner is all about personal growth. It is not a bitch session about spouses, children, and poverty. If you have trouble in those areas, you need more than a mastermind partner.

4. **Turn into a habitual personal planner.** If you cannot organize a party in a brewery, then you better get a grip on personal planning. Personal planning success is paramount to success as a leader.

   You need to have a solid and balanced personal plan that takes into account your:
   - Personal life
   - Professional life
   - Finances
   - Health and well-being for body, mind, and spirit

   I learned habitual discipline many years ago when I first crafted an annual personal plan for what I wanted to achieve in the next twelve months. Every year I create such a plan. I then break it down into what can I do to achieve a part of those goals in a month. I then further break it down every Sunday night with a weekly plan. When a plan is broken down into baby, bite-sized pieces, it is much easier to execute, and I get a huge thrill out of checking off my list each week!

Being a good personal planner is critical to being a great leader—if you don't know where you are going as an individual, how do you expect to be able to develop strategic plans for your business and expect people to follow you?

5. **Turn your commute into a university.** Whether you drive into the office or take public transit to a client site, your commute time can be filled with learning! Free podcasts abound and can be found on almost every topic imaginable. Always have something you are listening to that will expand your knowledge base. When I was in my thirties, I forgot I had a radio in my car because I always had a cassette tape on the go (cassette tapes are from the dinosaur days before CD's, MP3 players, and iPods).

6. **Always be reading something.** Stop watching television. Use the time that the mediocre population is wasting watching TV to read. Whether it is an old-fashioned paper book, tablet, or eReader, always have a book to read. I usually have a couple on the go, and depending on where I sit down at night, I pick up the book that is there and keep expanding and stretching my mind. Mix it up on the topics you read—it can get really boring if all you ever read are business books. (This one excluded, of course!)

7. **Stay abreast of business news and always be thinking, "If I were CEO of that organization, what would I do?"** Everyday, the online papers are full of the latest merger talks, results releases, market conditions, strategies, government issues, etc. Read them so you are up-to-date with current events; however, go much deeper. Read and analyze the situation. If you were the CEO, what would you do? What are the possible scenarios and outcomes? What are the threats and opportunities? What weaknesses would you work on

and what strengths would you capitalize on? Using your analytical muscle will strengthen your ability to develop strategies and solve problems.

8. **Do what you say you are going to do.** Nothing is more powerful than developing a personal brand of trust, meaning that you will always do what you say you will do. Sometimes, that means pulling an all night shift to deliver something (I once worked thirty-two hours straight in the office to deliver a projection on a business I was starting up). The world is full of people who accept deadlines, but then let them come and go without delivering or arranging alternative solutions. Delivering what you promise is a big skill to learn and master.

9. **Learn to say "No."** Sometimes, the hardest thing to learn is how to say "No." Young leaders feel that everyone is counting on them and that it will be a great project for their careers so they will try to take on the impossible. It takes massive learning to know what you can deliver on time and on budget and what you cannot. I see countless young leaders blowing their brains out while delivering mediocre projects because they have over-extended themselves.

   World-class athletes became the best in the world because they focused on what they wanted to be the best at, and they said, "No" to everything else. Reduce the clutter and focus on what you are good at. Say "No" to everything that distracts you from turning into being great at what you do. Saying "No" prevents you from delivering unparalleled mediocre crap.

10. **Go to workshops!** It drives me crazy when I see colleagues who are supposed to be at a development workshop sitting at their desks, say-

ing, "I am too busy to go!" It is a hazardous slope to give up training and development opportunities for yourself. Even if the topic seems lame or boring, I always go. I always find something in the presentation that I can use (even if it is "What not to do."). I always find that time away from my desk refreshes my thinking and allows me to come up with ideas and solutions for something back in the office.

Oops! Did I say there were 10? Here is a bonus tip:

11. **Learn the "sweetness of imperfection" in yourself and others.** This lesson is all about emotional intelligence. The kind of intelligence that comes from the recognition of what you are great at and what you may never be able to do. At forty years of age, I came to the realization that I would never be tall. That made me a better leader because I did not have to keep acting like I was. I was able to stop taking myself so seriously, and that opened my mind to my strengths versus continuous focus on my weaknesses.

The world is full of perfection and blemishes all at once—that is what makes it a great place. Did your mother give up trying to change you when you were a teenager, or did she just come to the realization that you were perfect the way you were? You were attracted to your partner because of the perfection you saw at the time. Learning always to appreciate the perfection in others and embrace the imperfection at the same time will give you the keen leadership ability to know who to put in the game at exactly the right time.

Don't get me wrong, I am still professing that you surround yourself with greatness in everyone. Hire people who are smarter than you. Hang out with people who have had more success, and always keeping pushing to go further. Just do it by admiring the strengths in others and appreciating their weaknesses too. You will get more people wanting to go with you on the journey.

CHAPTER 35

Create Cloud Time and Solve the World's Problems—At Least the Problems in Your World

"Time given to thought is the greatest timesaver of all."
— Norman Cousins

I came to the realization a number of years ago that I was far more productive at my job, far more strategic, and a far better leader when I carved out time in each day and during the business week to goof off! I call it "cloud time."

When you were a kid, did you ever lie flat out on a piece of grass and stare up at the clouds? You could see all sorts of shapes in the big, fluffy groups of cumulus nimbus overhead. Your friends would get in on the action and point out shapes and figures they saw. Our imaginations went wild!

Now that you are older, you are far too mature to goof off, and the pressures of the fancy job you think you have do not allow time for you to let your brain wonder pointlessly. "Life is far too serious for that!" you rationalize.

Have you ever noticed, however, how very difficult it is to solve complex problems while you are sitting at your desk? Yet, when you are standing in the shower—just standing there decompressing from a taxing day—answers to difficult problems come easily to you as if the water hitting you on the back of your tense neck has magical powers. The same thing happens to me when I am mowing the lawn, walking the dog, or washing my car. Weird, right? Not at all!

The funny part is that the answers have always been there, buried in the depths of our subconscious. The deepest recesses of our mind are a very powerful computer processor capable of solving the most complex problems with lightning speed. The issue, however, is that our conscious minds are so full of clutter with issues and stressors that we cannot hear the answers coming at us from the subconscious brain.

The answer is in creating "a quietness" in our minds so we can actually hear our own thoughts—the kind of quiet that comes when we are in the shower, or out for a run, or weeding the garden.

Mandated or organized cloud time for me comes in the daily form of getting up early when the house is quiet and just sitting by myself for about fifteen minutes. I don't do anything except maybe sip a cup of tea. Next, I get another forty-five minutes or so of daily cloud time when I head out the door for a run by myself. A walk would do the same thing—the dog would love it too! Whatever you do, you will be blown away by the clarity you get when you get in the habit of carving out time every morning to do nothing. Think about nothing. Just be. Don't force yourself to think. Just let it be and you will soon discover the subconscious will get messages through to you about innovative solutions and creative ideas.

For the next part, I know what you are going to say: "There is no hope in Hades that I am going to get away with having cloud time at work! You are truly smoking something! I have way too much stuff to do! My boss will have kittens!"

A long time ago, I had a boss subject to birthing small furry felines at the drop of a hat. I worked my tail off so I would not have to suffer the wrath of his tantrums about productivity, projects, and sales numbers. I started working harder—and longer hours. Still he gave me more abuse because I was not solving problems and getting things done. One day, out of complete frustration, I got up from my cubicle and walked out of the office. I strolled across the street and into the park for a walk around the small lake there. My plan was to figure out what to do when I got back to the office to face an immediate firing squad.

While I was out goofing off, stuff, really good stuff, started flowing in my stressed out mind. "Wow!" I thought, "This is unbelievable. I am a genius!" When I got back to the office, I discovered that the dictator did not even know I had been gone! I went into his office and shared my ideas with him. His face lit up. I think he may have even said something nice to me (although I doubt it). He asked me how I came up with the ideas? I told him I had just gone out for a walk. He replied by telling me to take walks more often. So I did.

My cloud time has evolved into a regularly scheduled two-hour time slot once a week in the middle of the morning. Every week, I take time to goof off for two hours. I go for a walk or a drive and just "be alone" with my subconscious innovation machine.

Cloud time has made me unbelievably productive in terms of problem-solving, developing new ideas, and innovative strategies.

For you, cloud time may look like a longer lunch or going for a walk after work. Whatever it is, do it! Get in the habit of getting up earlier, and at least once a week, goof off all by yourself for an hour or two. Once you do, stand back and be amazed!

Postscript: My tyrannical boss got fired a couple of years later when the company realized he was promoting my ideas as his own. I got promoted into his role.

> Challenge: Sit down with your calendar and carve out "Cloud Time" at least once a week. Stick to it and watch the creativity unfold in front of you!

CHAPTER 36

Everything Matters—Absolutely Everything

"Your work is going to fill a large part of your life, and the only way to be truly satisfied is to do what you believe is great work."

— Steve Jobs

A good friend of mine, Stewart Sonne, pointed out this very weird fact to me when we were talking about the subject of everything mattering. He said that the difference between the best golfer in the world and the tenth best, from any given season, is less than a stroke. But the difference in their take-home pay is in the millions. So I went online and researched it. What I found was fascinating.

In 2010, the difference between the winnings of the Professional Golfers Association's (PGA) number one golfer and the number ten golfer for the year was $1,335,927 with Matt Kuchar winning $4,910,476 for the year, and number ten, Hunter Mahan winning $3,574,549. They both played the same number of tournaments for the year and they both shot approximately the same number of rounds of golf. Yet, remarkably, the difference in the average score for the year was only 0.3. Kuchar shot an average of 69.7 and Mahan shot an average of 70.0. Less than a shot on average separated them by over a million dollars!

What was the difference? Kuchar was ever so marginally better on the greens with his putter. Everything matters!

My friend Stewart lives by the concept that everything matters. Stewart is a senior leader in the public education system where I live. Stewart saw a trend in graduation numbers a few years back and decided to lead a program to change the downward trend. In the school year 2005-2006, the graduation rate among Grade 12 students in his district was 78.12 percent. A quarter of the kids were dropping out of school and not graduating! Stewart put a program in place to make school a place where kids wanted to be so they would graduate. Six years later, in the 2010-2011 school year, the graduation rate had risen to 88.71 percent! The improvement was amazing!

Here's the part I like about everything mattering. The difference in the graduation rate meant that fifty or so more kids graduated than would have five years earlier. Those fifty kids will now go on to getting higher paid jobs. They will establish a higher standard of living for fifty families that will produce approximately one hundred children. Statistics show that those one hundred children will grow up in a more stable family environment and receive a higher level of education themselves, which in turn will make them more competitive in the marketplace so they can achieve more. The cycle goes on and on. And it all started with Stewart wanting more kids to graduate. Everything matters!

Everything you do in your life and as a leader matters. Everything. How much sleep you get. How much exercise. What you put into your body. Your education. Your continuing education. How you treat other people at home, at work, and on the street. The list goes on and on.

The key thing, though, is understanding that all that has gone into you to this point in time matters. All that goes into you from this moment forward matters. Here are ten key areas you can ensure matter most for you and your leadership package:

1. **Skill and Will.** Heavyweight champion Muhammad Ali once said, "There are those with the skill and those with the will but true champions have the skill and the will. And I believe that the will is more important." As an ice hockey coach, I have lost track of how many kids I have met with unbelievable natural talent but no drive to be the best. They never go anywhere in the sport. The kids, however, who come to me with little skill, but a burning, unquenchable desire to learn and be the best, have always gone further in the game.

2. **Pledge to be the very best in the world at what you do.** Of all the business people, entrepreneurs, and leaders in the world, 97 percent are mediocre. The other 3 percent make more money than the 97 percent put together. Those 3 percent all share the same trait: a burning desire to be the best. They have life plans with documented goals and objectives. They accept nothing less for themselves than being the very best they can be. They get up early and make things happen while everyone else is sleeping. Like the world's number one golfer in 2010, the difference is being better at putting, or whatever your focus or business may be.

No matter what your job is or what level you are in the company, be the very best at it. Ask yourself, "If I were the very best in the world at this, what would I be doing right now?" Basketball great Larry Bird talks about how every single time he lay down in bed, he visualized in his mind every minuscule detailed step to making a perfect free-throw basket. Michael Jordan's dad quite often would wake up in the middle of the night to the thump, thump, thump of a basketball and discover his son outside shooting hoops. Wayne Gretzky's dad had to turn out the lights to the backyard ice arena to get his son to come inside at night. U.S. President Obama was a terrible speaker as President of the Harvard Law Society. Today, he is revered as one of the best orators in the world—that did not happen by accident.

3. **Protect your name.** Your name and your reputation take years, maybe even decades, to build, but only seconds to destroy. As a leader, you are always on a stage and under a microscope. You cannot for a single instant do anything that is not aligned with who you are and your values. Ever.

4. **Protect your brand.** Next time you find yourself wandering the aisles of a grocery store, be very conscious of the multiple different brands there are for the same thing. There must be over a hundred different cereal brands. What makes you pick a particular brand off the shelf? If you turned down the next aisle and that was where they keep the "Leaders," and you came to the box on the shelf that had you inside, what would make someone take you down and purchase you? Make a list of all the things that make up your brand. My list is made up of single words like "Authentic. Innovative. Integrity. Motivational. Determined. Visionary. Focused. Courageous. Results." I never violate my brand essence. Ever.

5. **Dress for success.** Always dress for the job you want to have, not the one you have. Make sure your clothes are the best you can afford and impeccably tailored and clean. Your shoes are polished. Your personal hygiene is first class. Every human on the planet makes an entire assessment of you within the first three seconds he or she meets you. Those first impressions are hard to change. Carry yourself with pride and confidence. When you meet people for the first time, be the first to offer your hand. Look people in the eye, and as soon as you can, repeat the person's name back to him to show you care about him enough to remember his name.

6. **Say "Please" and "Thank you" a lot.** Good manners are rare in business today and rarely used. As a leader, you will get more people to follow your visions and strategies when they willingly want to come on the journey. Impressing upon your people that you truly care about them goes most of the way to building trust. Saying, "Please" means "I respect you." Saying, "Thank you" means "I appreciate you." When I am with a group of people, I will often get the comment about how I get better service than someone else— "You are lucky," they say. Luck has nothing to do with it. I never fail to say "Please" and I always say "Thank you," no matter how small the request or act is.

7. **Learn to "serve."** The most successful leaders on the planet have figured out that that they are lifelong servants. Servitude is something that comes easily when you let go of your ego. It does not make you less of a leader. It makes you stronger. What I mean by "serve" consists of simple things like:
   - Serve your team coffee and muffins at their desks every once in awhile.

- When an elevator door opens, let your team get on before you. I always hold a door open for anyone on my team; let him order first at a restaurant or let her go through a doorway first. If your team members hesitate, I simply say, "I am overhead; you actually make this business successful."
- Challenge yourself to connect with an employee every day by asking him questions about his work and what ideas he has to make the business better or his job easier.
- Once every six months, do a 2 x 2 x 2 x 2 feedback. That is, get your team together and hand out blank cards. Ask the team to write down:
    - Two things they like about your leadership style
    - Two things they do not like about your leadership style
    - Two things they like about the company
    - Two things they do not like about the company

Ask someone to collect the finished cards and then leave the room so confidentiality is assured. Act on the feedback you get back. The list goes on and on. If you want to be the very best leader possible, learn to serve. And that does not stop when you get a corner office with a view.

8. **Do nice things for others even if they never find out.** I had this happen to me in Florence, Italy. My son and I were standing in line for ice cream at a gelato parlour. When it was our turn to order, we both ordered a yummy dark chocolate scoop of creamy goodness in a waffle cone. When I pulled out my wallet to pay, the server said with a thick Italian accent, "The couple in front of you already paid for you." I was completely dumbfounded! It took me a few seconds to comprehend what had happened. Then I quickly looked around to thank the generous benefactors but they were gone. Now I make it a habit to put coins into a parking meter that has expired—once I

even stopped a parking attendant from ticketing a car whose time had expired by paying for another hour of parking. The attendant asked me why I would do that for someone I didn't know. I simply replied, "Someone did that for me in Italy and this car may be theirs."

9. **Walk a mile in someone else's shoes.** It is an old cliché, but a highly effective reminder to all leaders to make a point of truly understanding their audiences. When you are able to understand what is important to other people, you will become a better negotiator, parent, spouse, partner, coach, teammate, businessperson, and leader. You will save hours of time and frustration leading change management processes.

10. **You are what you put into your mind and your body.** No further narrative needed on this one. What you put into your brain determines your ability to think and reason with others. What you put into your body determines whether you will perform like a world-class champion at what you do or whether you will be one of the majority who are languishing in mediocrity.

Final Thoughts...

I have been a leader for a long time. It does come easier to me now than it used to. I am still a work in progress though, and I will be all my life. I have had lots of mentors and influences along the way. I have read a few hundred books on leadership. I have taken all of the best of the best leadership lessons I have received and put them here for you to grow from.

Peak leadership is already inside. You have it in you. There is no magic wand to bring it out or Kool-Aid you can drink so you wake up tomorrow as a world-class leader who can get people to dance to music that has yet to be written. It takes hard work and practice. Lots of practice. Lots of mistakes.

And, you need to become a student and teacher of leadership. The world's best leaders got where they did through learning and teaching.

The thirty-six chapters you have just come through form the foundational imperatives for your leadership development. This book should become a reference for your future use as a leader and as a mentor to others.

Develop your life plan and start to execute on it. You will soon be amazed by how things start to fall into place.

Make sure your life is balanced and you factor fun, adventure, and love into your life. The road to the top (however you define that) can be very lonely because there are not a lot of people on the same road. Having a balanced life will make the journey an amazing one. Having a balanced life, however, takes conscious thought—otherwise work and projects will fill in your available time. Having love, friendship, and harmony in your life takes conscious thought too. Great relationships don't just happen (That's called "Lust"); they take effort, creative thought, and commitment. Great relationships are not a one-way street.

Make sure your plan has elements built in for you, your body, your brain, and your spirit. If you, as an individual, are not operating at a peak level, you will be mediocre as a leader, friend, family member, and partner to someone.

Life will throw you challenges. Some days it will feel like the challenges are all lined up and you are the complaint department! That is inevitable. You can choose to have a pity party or you can choose to rise up as a leader who looks for opportunities in everything and move forward. The pages you have just read will help you develop the skill to see the opportunity and focus on the solution. Remember, greatness is already inside you.

Get out there and lead, have fun, and enjoy the success that is going to come your way!

RECOMMENDED READING

Friedman, Thomas L. *The World is Flat 3.0: A Brief History of the Twenty-First Century*. New York: Farrar, Straus, & Giroux, 2007.

Gladwell, Malcolm. *The Tipping Point: How Little Things Can Make a Big Difference*. New York: Little, Brown and Company, 2000.

Godin, Seth. *Purple Cow: Transform Your Business by Being Remarkable*. New York: Penguin, 2003.

Godin, Seth. *The Dip: A Little Book that Teaches You When to Quit (and When to Stick)*. New York: Penguin, 2007.

Hsieh, Tony. *Delivering Happiness: A Path to Profits, Passion, and Purpose*. New York: Hachette Book Group, 2010.

Kim, W. Chan and Renée Mauborgne. *Blue Ocean Strategy: How to Create Uncontested Market Space and Make Competition Irrelevant*. Boston: Harvard, 2005.

Kriegel, Robert. *Sacred Cows Make the Best Burgers: Developing Change-Driving People and Organizations*. New York: Warner Books, 1996.

Morrison, Terri and Wayne Conaway. *Kiss, Bow, or Shake Hands (The Bestselling Guide to Doing Business in More than 60 Countries)*. Avon, MA: Adams Media, 2006.

Parker, James F. *Do the Right Thing: How Dedicated Employees Create Loyal Customers and Large Profits*. Upper Saddle River, NJ: Wharton School Publishing, 2008.

Sharma, Robin. *The Leader Who Had No Title: A Modern Fable on Real Success in Business and in Life.* New York: Free Press, 2010.

Sisodia, Raj, Jag Sheth and David B. Wolfe. *Firms of Endearment: How World-Class Companies Profit from Passion and Purpose.* Upper Saddle River, NJ: Wharton School Publishing, 2007.

Turner, Natasha. *The Hormone Diet: A 3-Step Program to Help You Lose Weight, Gain Strength, and Live Younger Longer.* Toronto, CA: Random House, 2009.

Any children's book you can read with your own children, nieces, nephews, or friend's children.

ABOUT THE AUTHOR

Robert Murray lives in Vancouver, Canada with his amazing wife of over twenty-seven years, Colleen, their two children, Denielle and Grant, and a crazy Border Collie named Jasper.

Bob has spent a lifetime studying and learning authentic leadership—beyond just taking a group of people from "Point A" to "Point B," he takes the whole person within the leader and nurtures the whole leader from the inside out.

Currently, Bob is:

- Partner at Incrementa Consulting — A Vancouver based group of unique multidiciplinary experts, brought togheter by a shared passion for helping businesses be successful.
- An Advisory Board Member of ElementFour (an organization that has developed a technology to produce pure, potable drinking water from atmospheric air).
- An Associate Professor on Strategy, Marketing, and Leadership at British Columbia Institute of Technology's School of Business in Vancouver.
- A passionate speaker on leadership and strategy in life and business.

For information on how you can book Bob to come to your organization or next event to speak about *It's Already Inside*, visit **www.Robert-Murray.com**

Printed in the USA
CPSIA information can be obtained
at www.ICGtesting.com
JSHW022219140824
68134JS00018B/1158